Samson and His Women

Keys to Getting Right

What You Keep Getting Wrong

Your Personal Guide: From Courtship to Marriage

Dr. Robert E. Kimble

Dr. Robert E. Kimble

Dedication

First, let me thank posthumously, the late Deacon Jewell C. Lockhart Sr. for believing and saying that I would write my first book over 20 years ago. Thank God for your vision.

To my children (Shawn, Shevette, Symone, and Simeon) and my grandchildren (Shaquana, Ayanna, Shayne, Makayla, and Simeon Jr.)

I dedicate this book to you with my profound faith, love, and best wishes for God's divine favor upon you. The Lord bless and keep you; the Lord make His face shine upon you, be gracious, and give you peace. (Numbers 6:24-26).

About the Author

Robert E. Kimble, a respected figure in faith, currently serving as Pastor of New Hope First Baptist in Greenville, Mississippi. Besides his role as a retired Allstate agent and educator, Kimble has a rich educational background. He studied at Mississippi Valley State University for his bachelor's degree and pursued further studies at Jackson State University, Jackson, Mississippi.

Kimble's dedication to spiritual education led him to earn a Certificate of Theology from ITC, Atlanta, GA, along with an M.Div. and a Doctor of Divinity from Slidell Baptist Seminary, Slidell, La. Currently, he serves as the State Evangelist for the General Missionary Baptist State Convention of Mississippi, where he's highly sought after as a speaker and educator.

Kimble is deeply committed to spreading the gospel and the teachings of Jesus Christ globally. His passion lies in making a positive impact on the world, and sharing the message of faith in simple and understandable ways.

Acknowledgment

I am grateful to the many who encouraged me to venture into this writing project. It has been my lifelong dream and desire. I am highly indebted to my parents, the late Dr. & Mrs. J. M. and Jeretha Kimble. They adopted me from an orphanage in Little Rock, Arkansas. Without God's divine providence, I would despise to think how my story would have ended. To God be the glory for the things He has done. My dad was my mentor who taught me much about God and His glorious Kingdom. He was my Paul, and he transformed me into his Timothy.

I have nothing but heaps of thanks to the five churches that facilitated my spiritual growth and development. They are Mount Beulah of Indianola, Mississippi; Pleasant Valley of Inverness, MS; Southdale of Anguilla, MS; New Hope First Baptist, Greenville, MS, and the church where I have served as pastor for the past 25+ years.

I am what I am because of the great people who allowed me to grow and develop my craft as an evangelist, preacher, and pastor. Thank God for the expedition. It has been an incredible experience indeed.

After I retired from Allstate Insurance Company, I taught Social Studies in various school districts in the Mississippi Delta for a decade. In that process, I am indebted to the many who influenced my life. I want to recognize three co-workers who meant the world to me: Mrs. Takisha Williams, Mrs. Keshia Phillips, and Miss Marilyn Patty, my cousin on my wife's side, who helped me keep it together as an aspiring educator. Thank you so much for your prayers, support, and jovial spirit.

Last but not least, I want to thank my wife, Carol. We have been married for 35 years. I will never figure out why she loves me so much and puts up with me, but I am happy she does. She helps me look good despite my shortcomings, especially in technology. She is my executive chef, cheerleader, companion, and coach. I love you so much!

God is the one who inspired me to write this book on strategies and biblical skills for a better marriage and human relationships, and as I say to my church when I am about to preach, "Let the words of my mouth and the meditation of my heart be acceptable in thy sight, O Lord, my strength and my redeemer." (Psalm 19:14).

Table of Contents

Introduction

Samson is a biblical story filled with sex, money, power, betrayal, and suspense. It reads like a soap opera straight out of Hollywood. It has its protagonist (Samson) and the antagonists (Samson's women and the Philistines). It is filled with the loved and unloved, and betrayer and betrayed. It is a biblical account that answers all relationships' pressing and complicated challenges. Hopefully, you will discover some solutions.

Everything in the Bible is true, but everything is **Not** correct. It is accurate that Adam and Eve ate the fruit of the Tree of Knowledge of good and evil. However, it was not right to disobey God. King David indeed loved Bathsheba, but it was not right that he got her pregnant and had her husband killed; Uriah, to take her as his wife. Life is short; we must learn to get things right and what we keep doing wrong.

Samson had a difficult time choosing the right type of girlfriend and in fact, he never did. We should look in depth as to why he made bad choices. What should we do differently? What paths can we follow that will lead to success? God has all the answers in His Word.

As a pastor for over 25 years, I have encountered a lot of hurt and confusion regarding relationships. I see couples who argue and fight all the time and claim they love each other and want to live their lives together, only to find that they are caught up in domestic violence and unhappiness. The list is never-ending. Today's courtship scene is far different than what I grew up with. I have children, and I have watched them struggle with the desire to find happiness and fulfillment. It is frustrating to see them searching for answers. So, I decided to help. I want to share a few things that I have discovered along the way. I dare not say that all I say is watertight, bulletproof, or the secret sauce to happiness.

However, if what I share on these pages is taken seriously and with an open mind and heart, it will move you closer to your goal—to find and develop a long and lasting relationship with the one you love. The idea of this book is to look behind the scenes of a man named Samson from Chapter 1 through Chapter 7. From Chapters 8 to 14, my focus shifts to providing a practical and portable guide designed to offer resolutions to the single and searching and those married—promoting better and healthier outcomes.

The goal in life should be to maximize our potential and minimize our failures. We can do that by learning from others' mistakes. If we can learn how to harness wisdom from the past and the synergy of scriptures, we can fly higher and farther. I hope this book will make it happen for you.

Before we examine the life of Samson, let's first review God's original design for man and how quickly things got out of hand. Israel's sin brings Samson onto the scene many centuries into the future.

The law first calls our attention to Adam and Eve of the Bible. They had the burden of being the first couple in the world. Adam had never been the man of the house, and Eve had to learn to be a wife and mother at the same time. They had no model for their lives or relationships because they were the world's first family. What do you do when a baby starts crying? This was a challenging circumstance for them. Furthermore, they had an enormous responsibility in their example of love, faith, obedience, and populating the earth while cultivating and beautifying Paradise.

I genuinely believe that Eve persuaded Adam to eat the forbidden fruit using manipulation as a tactic that Delilah might have used: "If you love me, you will ….." This turned out to be a devastating proposition. We all can identify with the Adam and Eve love story because we all have transgressed at some point and fallen prey to the lust of the eyes, the flesh, and the pride of life. **(1 John 2:16)**

Adam was the viceroy of God and was commissioned to name every living thing. With all his intelligence, no one was found suitable for him. God, therefore, created a helpmate for him. Eve was created from Adam's rib. We find it recorded in the Bible: the first anesthesia performed in the world was on Adam. God put him to sleep, and when he woke him up, as a father gives a daughter away at marriage, God the Father brought Eve to Adam. They became the world's first couple. Adam called her Wo-man or WOOOO-man! You get the picture.

Allow me to chronicle and catalog a few of the demerits they racked up. Eve was approached by an upright creature, a serpent who misguided her, and she ate the fruit of the Tree of Knowledge of good and evil and gave Adam the fruit also. As a result, they lost their beautiful estate in Eden and were exiled. The first book of the Bible records the world's foremost institution, the family, and before the book of Genesis closes, even before the world gets started for good, the very first book of the Bible ends with a funeral in Egypt.

Sin and disobedience start their march across the pages of Jewish history. This theme will show up time and time again. God's desire for the world's first couple was to live life to get things right. Instead, they experienced death, decay, and spiritual separation from each other and God. We will never know just all the things they lost. Adam and Eve never got a chance to get things right what they got wrong.

Adam was God's dream then, and man is still God's dream now. God wants us to learn from our predecessors and learn to get things right what we keep getting wrong in our relationship with God and each other. The fall of Adam and Eve brought distrust among themselves, fear, and insecurity because of disobedience. The home and harmony of Adam and Eve never were the same after they sinned, and God would have to send a redeemer to restore, not only for them but for the whole world, the Paradise they lost, through his Son, Christ Jesus.

Let us focus on the Nation of Israel and see how humans struggle with love, deception, rejection, lewdness, and the like. I know that you will be helped and enlightened and learn a better approach as we contemplate the failures of the first family and the cycles of sin that ultimately caused God to bring Samson to the stage of history.

To fully understand the Nation of Israel, we would do well to observe the sinful state they found themselves in. They were no longer captive to the deserts and melons of Egypt. Moses, the great emancipator, had delivered them, and Joshua continued to press on into the promised land. Sadly, they came out of Egypt but never got Egypt out of them!

They were called to be a Holy Nation, a called-out people. They were strong, courageous, and filled with hope until Joshua died. He had no successor. This was a critical mistake, and the people were now leaderless. Success always needs a successor. After the death of Joshua, everything seemed to take a nosedive.

The people had no moral compass, they had no king, and they made up their own rules. In the truest sense, every man did what was right in their eyes. **(Judges 21:25)** They went through the cycles of sin. When Israel served God, peace and prosperity were abundant in the land. When Israel did evil in the land, God punished Israel, and they found themselves enslaved. Israel cried out to God for deliverance, and God raised a judge. The judge, at last, delivered Israel, and they went back through the cycle all over and again. God gave them some form of stability by providing them with judges whose duty was to remind them of God's way and not their own.

Israel was constantly sinful. What is sin? In simple words, sin is anything contrary to the law of God. A negative impulse in man's heart motivates and moves man to escape from the law of God and His righteousness. The book of Judges is the saga of sin on display. History repeats itself. The characters are the same. The only thing that appears to be different is the characters' costumes.

You may be wondering, "Why is sin so attractive?" Or is it really? I suggest the world labels and reclassifies sin as a more attractive enterprise. We want to make ourselves feel better about doing wrong. The reason why we gravitate toward sin is that the underlying problem is an unmet need. We seek to meet a legitimate need through illegitimate means. The devil tells us that it will make us happy and pleasure us. Then our flesh kicks in and goes into overdrive. We have always mistaken wants for needs. As the saying goes, we pay for what we want and beg for what we need!

I taught social studies for a decade. During that time, I taught economics, a concept called "Guns and Butter," a theory of opportunity cost. Everything we do has an opportunity cost—everything, and I mean everything. For every choice we make, we sacrifice something. A country cannot produce unlimited guns because it needs butter. Therefore, we must make choices regardless of how many guns and how much butter will be produced. Since we do not have unlimited resources, we must limit the production of goods and services. That said, we must make the right choices every day. Our lifespan is limited, and we must make the right choices because we will eventually spend eternity with God or the devil.

Moreover, God raised judges to keep the peoples' minds on making the right choices. I want to think of the role of a judge in Israel's history as a type of Andy Griffith of Mayberry. Andy had a dual role if I remember correctly. He was the sheriff as well as the justice of the peace. The Judges of Israel had a dual role as well. They performed the duties of a law-and-order person (military leader) and a domestic person to see after civic affairs.

Judges 13 begins with the domination of the Philistines that dogged Israel for 40 years nonstop. However, all judges were not men. Deborah was the only exception. She stood tall as a prophetess and a defender of Israel and strategically defeated the wicked Canaanites.

The first judge was Othniel. In all, there will be 12 judges in Israel. Samson is destined to become the last judge: a champion and a super-strong man.

Chapter One

Here Comes the Judge

Samson had his work cut out for him. He was God's chosen and had a tremendous responsibility. It was up to him to be the vessel to honor God's demands and be a spiritual leader for the people and defend them.

The marching orders of God were pretty simple; all the people of God had to do was take the land before them and drive out the inhabitants; then, they would enjoy living under trees they did not plant and houses they did not build. The challenge was ridding the land of all those Canaanites, Perizzites, and Hittites. Moses, the great lawgiver, provided standards to live by, but they constantly disobeyed them. However, before we begin to lash out at them so swiftly, people worldwide have been calling God's word unholy since the beginning of time as well irreverent.

The Jews did not do what the Lord commanded, and so they were constantly harassed by their enemies, particularly the Philistines. We cannot compromise with the world. We must stand our ground. If we do not, we will suddenly find our safety and serenity shifting from over our heads and underneath our feet.

Samson is the epitome of everything antithetical to the royal law of God. Most men dream of finding a devout wife so that God's richest blessings will follow their lifelong journey of matrimony. Samson's life is a textbook case of how not to find a wife. This book aims to examine the biblical account of some of the pitfalls Samson fell into and discover God's design for finding a God-given mate and using those keys.

We all remember Superman, Clark Kent incognito, born on the planet Krypton, with superhuman strength, whose mission is to fight crime and the underworld crime bosses. Amazingly, in the comic genre, he had four women who had a crush on him, according to an article by Jessie Greenspan of the History Channel, "Eight Things You May Not Know About Superman." Their initials were LL, Lois Lane, a reporter drawn by his meek ego. There is Lana Lang, a high school sweetheart from Smallville, Kansas. Lori Lemaris, a mermaid he dates while a student at Metropolis University, and Lyla Lerrol, an aspiring actress from Krypton who meets him when he travels back before the planet's ultimate destruction. Superman had four women to chase after him, with the massive "S" on his chest. Samson is the biblical superhero version of the comic hero Superman.

In addition, Samson had three women that he chased. Three were serious pursuits; if there were others, they were causal. He had an invisible "S" on his chest! Now, mind you, Samson had a weakness. As you recall, cutting his hair would render him weak and powerless. Superman also had a weakness. Superman's weakness was kryptonite, a radioactive substance that makes the man of steel vulnerable to enemy attack. So, now you know the commonalities of these superheroes at last!

In the contemporary world, Samson would be listed on the roster of the U.S. Olympic team, voted most likely to succeed on adorning Sports Illustrated page flexing his muscles. However, Samson will be governed by his lustful eyelids and his passions.

The Life of Samson is an open-book exam of how the best of us can drift away from our divine purpose. **Hebrews 2:1** says, "We must pay the most careful attention, therefore, to what we have heard, so that we do not drift away." Samson was guilty of drifting big time. Samson reminds me of an old song that a spirit-filled old lady sang live on the radio broadcast in the Mississippi Delta every Sunday morning in Greenville, MS, called the Taborian Hour. The title of the song was

"Without God, I Could Do Nothing," written by Beatrice Brown. The lady who loved to sing this song was Mary Williams, and boy, oh boy, could she sing it! The lyrics went something like this:

Yes,

Without God, I could do nothing, Oh, Lord

Without God, you know all my life would fail

Without God, my life would be rugged, Oh Lord,

Yes, like a ship (like a ship)

Without a sail, without a sail, (Without a sail)

Mmmmm

Without a doubt, he is my Savior,

Yes, my strength, along, along life's waves

Yes, In deep waters, my God, he is my anchor

Lord, & through faith he'll keep me always

Yeah, Without God, I could do nothing, Praise God

Without God, you know my life would fail Mmmm

Without God, Life would be rugged, Oh Lord

It'd be like a ship (like a ship)

Without a sail (without a sail)

Mmmmm

I'm leanin' and dependin' on Jesus

And I'm trustin in him everyday

I'm waitin', I'm just waitin' for my for my Savior

Because one of these old days he gonna dry all my tears away

Yeah, yeah,

Without God, I could do nothin', Praise the Lord

Without him, do you know my life would fail,

Hmmm Lord

Without God, my life would be rugged, Oh Lord

Yes like a ship (like a ship)

Without (without a sail) a sail

Samson was a ship without a sail, drifting further into the rocks of sin. Hebrews 2:1 says, "We must pay the most careful attention, therefore, to what we have heard, so that we do not drift away." The verb in Hebrews 2:1 means to "flow or drift alongside or by." It carries the idea of allowing the currents of the waters to carry us away from a fixed point of reference by carefree attitudes and carelessness, with little or no concern. Instead of Samson keeping a firm grip on the sails of his life, he drifts and finds himself in enemy territory, enjoying deadly folly.

Let us be fair; he is not the only one in scripture to drift. Lot ended up in Sodom by turning his antennas toward Sodom and picking up lewd pictures on the screen of his mind. David is another. Had he been at war on the battlefield where he should have been, rather than on the rooftop of his penthouse, he never would have committed adultery with Bathsheba.

The disciples drifted because of their fear of the Romans and the horrors of crucifixion. But the key is to pay attention. We can end up in a shipwreck when we do not keep abreast of the facts. We must pay attention to our relationships. We must keep watch over the road signs. They may say "One Way," "Dead End," or "Bridge out." Whatever the case, we must pay attention to the signs on the roads of life we travel and stay off Broadway! **Matthew 7:13-14** says, "Enter by the narrow gate; for wide *is* the gate and broad *is* the way that leads to destruction, and many go in by it. [14] [a]Because narrow *is* the gate and [b]difficult *is* the way which leads to life, and there are few who find it."

The key to staying focused is to look unto Jesus, the author and finisher of our faith. **(Hebrews 12:2)**

Moreover, the life of Samson should motivate and inspire those who are single and searching to be prayerful and follow the leading of the Holy Spirit and not let the desires of the flesh be the umpire. The Bible says, "for he that soweth to his flesh shall of the flesh reap corruption; but he that soweth to the Spirit shall of the Spirit reap life everlasting." **(Gal 6:8)**

If we place Samson and his women in a particular category, it could easily be *the hopeless romantics*, recorded and cataloged in **BRIDE, November 16, 2022.** They are described as a love that ignites and burns out fast, a one-sided relationship, and overly optimistic.

The parents of Samson were from the town of Zorah. His birth was miraculous; his mother was barren, and the Angel of the Lord appeared to the wife of Manoah, Zealphonis, according to the Talmud. This appearance is what Bible scholars call a Christophany. There are numerous accounts in the Bible of Christophanies. To mention a few, angels appeared to **Abraham, Gen.18:10; Gen 18:17, Gen 22:11.** They appeared to **Moses, Exod. 3:4-5, Exod. 23:20, Exod. 33:22.** They appeared to the **Three Hebrew Boys Dan. 3:24-25.**

To be barren in that part of the world meant that a woman was always subject to the danger of being divorced by a husband who wanted a son. It also meant that when her husband died, she would be alone and destined for poverty. A man would not willingly marry a woman who was known to be barren. It was a hard, harsh life to be a barren woman indeed.

According to the computation of time, Manoah's wife was told that when she would give birth to a son, his hair would not be cut, and he could not consume strong drinks or touch a dead thing. These were the requirements for a Nazarite vow. These prohibitions were unusual because they called for Samson to be a Nazarite from birth until death.

Most vows of this nature were only for a short period, usually about 30 days. The mother of Samson was also prohibited from touching any unclean thing or drinking strong drinks.

In Chapter 13, Samson's father shows great skepticism when told by his wife that an Angel had visited her and brought the news of the birth of a son. She told her husband how he was to be raised. Manoah was so doubtful that he prayed that the Angel would return and assure him it was true. His prayer was answered, and He knew God was in the plan.

Manoah exhibited mistrust of his wife and thought she was telling wild tales. I can understand that; I get it. Trust in marriage is foundational and can only lead to more insecurities. Such insecurities can impact the stability and outlook of children, as we will see in the life of Samson as he grows to adulthood.

Samson means "sun," after a pagan god of the Canaanites. You will see he is the "Sunny Boy" whose life grows darker and darker. Here begins the great contrast between fleshly power and spiritual power. Samson's dangerous weakness stems from a desire for strange women driven by emotions, lust of the eyes, lust of the flesh, and the pride of life. These inclinations were nothing new. Even before the flood, Jewish men wanted ungodly women.

In I Kings 11:1-2 King Solomon's marriage to foreign wives led to his separation from serving Yahweh in his quest for power, territory, pleasure, and peace. But it's all about compromise. Whenever we compromise, we give up something to gain something else. That something else is not always something we can live with. So be very careful.

Furthermore, the Life of Samson should cause us to examine ourselves personally as we take inventory of our relationship with the Lord and our relationship with the Holy Spirit working in our lives.

The prospect of finding a wife or a husband and those necessary character traits that we should long for and those we should reject should be established before we head out on this adventure. You have to know what you want; if not, there is no telling what might end up in your arms and your bedroom.

My mother was a home economist who taught homemakers never to go grocery shopping without a thoughtful grocery list. Without it, you will grab everything but what you need. You must know what your standards are. You must know what you are looking for when you are single and searching because, in your uncertainty, you will grab just about anything.

In addition, the spiritual principles we want to instill in our children should also be considered when choosing a mate. Both partners should share common beliefs. The Bible says, "Train up a child in the way he should go, and when he is old, they will not depart from it." **(Proverbs 22:6)**

Samson chooses three Philistine women; all have questionable characters. Building a successful life is all about making the right choices. The more information we have, the better choices we can make. We should be able to increase the positive and decrease the negative. Samson had adequate information to make better decisions. Let's take a look at Samson's first surprising choice.

Chapter Two

Samson's Girlfriend #1

The Tasmanian Devil

When I think about Samson's girlfriend #1, I think of the advertisement for GM's 2000 Chevy Monte Carlo SS years ago. The car comes down the street enclosed in a tornado, and a Tasmanian Devil appears when it stops. He puts a coin in the parking meter and touches the car with his thumb as he sees his reflection shining on the door. He reaches out to touch it with admiration and shouts, **"HOT."** Samson was about to give a thumbs up to a girl in the village who said "hot" as she caught his eye in Timnah, six miles from his hometown of Zorah. Timnah was located about halfway between Joppa (a coastal town on the Mediterranean Sea) and Jerusalem. Today, the small village is not occupied, and there is barely a trace that it ever existed.

Samson was like a restless bird that couldn't wait to spread his wings and fly from the nest. What was it in Timnah? Was it the swag of the girl? Was it her perfume in the air? Or her promiscuous street belly dance that captured his imagination? Whatever it was, it captivated him.

Samson picked his first girlfriend from a family of his enemies, the Philistines. The Philistines were called an uncircumcised people with advancements in technology, iron tools, and a mighty military front **(Judges 14:3; 1 Samuel 13:19–20; Exodus 13:17)**. The Philistines frequently trampled on Israel's territory, which led to many confrontations, including the famous clash between David, the Israelite, and Goliath, the Philistine. **(1 Samuel 17)** The Philistines were strongly condemned for being idol worshippers of the God

Dagon **(Joshua 19:27;1 Samuel 5:1–5)** and soothsayers. **(Isaiah 2:6)** They were also known to be superstitious.

Bullies, that is what the Philistines were. They were the ones that wanted to dominate the playground. They were a no-nonsense kind of folk. We have our cultural wars today, but they also had their share of wars. The Canaanites greatly influenced their religion. Keep in mind that the Israelites were agrarian people. They were just country farmers, and the Philistines were the heavy-weight wrestlers of their day. They were aggressive as well as rough and tough. This largely explains their bullying attitudes using fear and intimidation on their enemies.

In Judges 14, it appears that the Lord guided Samson's actions in some unexplained ways. The Bible says, "His parents did not know that this was from the Lord, who was seeking an occasion to confront the Philistines; for at that time, they were ruling over Israel."

Samson was a restless man and went sightseeing. Josephus, the Jewish historian, said a festival was happening in town. I would liken it to a carnival in our present age, a type of circus. In my imagination, I hear the music, and I see the painted faces and the booths, and a Philistine girl out shaking her rump in the streets to lure patrons to her booth, and so, Samson became a paying customer. The flashing dress, tingling bracelets, long hair, sweet-smelling perfume, lipstick, and long eyelashes were all too good to pass up. Samson was under her spell. The KJV says Samson went down to Timnath. **(Judges 14:1)** This is not just from a geographical sense; he went down spiritually and morally. The Bible also says Jonah went down to Joppa. **(Jonah 1:3)** Here, again, was an unfavorable pattern. Jonah went down and ended up in a whale of trouble! So, here we go again.

Now, Josephus also gives us insight into the home life of Samson. Josephus says his mother was very beautiful, and his father was very possessive and suspicious of her. He monitored her goings and comings whenever she went to town. This behavior helps us to understand Samson's questionable behavior when it comes to women.

Do men model what they see at home? They sure do, in love and in violence. Statistics repeatedly prove that boys who exhibit violent or rebellious behavior model what they see at home, school, and married life. Every Christian man should want to exhibit Godly behavior in an ungodly world.

I further suggest that when men are excessively suspicious of their wives' indiscretions, it indicates that the husband may also have some secret stuff going on.

So, after Samson saw this girl, he returned home from Timnah. He was excited, couldn't eat or sleep, and developed a must-have attitude. So, he said to his parents, "Go, get her for me. I want her; she pleases me well!" But here is the problem: she is a Philistine girl in the enemy camp. This was not acceptable and outside the covenant of Israel. His parents objected, but he said so what? This strained the family relationship and what they knew to be against God, but they were unaware that this was God's design. **(Judges 14: V4)**

It was against God's will for an Israelite to marry a Philistine, **Ex. 34:16; Deut. 7:3; Josh. 23:12**. Samson only cared about what made him happy and feel good, and he lived his life to please himself and not God.

Samson's desires stood in direct opposition to the will of God. This should have been a red flag to Samson. After all, he was to live out his entire life as "*a Nazarite to God*," **Jud. 13:7** he was to be "*separated unto the Lord*" for his entire life. His life was not his to do with as he pleased. His life was in the Lord's hand to use as He saw fit. We, too, have been bought with a price, and the redeemed belong to God. **(1 Cor: 6:20)** We are not our own; we have been bought with a price.

Samson's initial misstep was a distraction. He got distracted by a pretty girl and went astray from his God-given task: to be a leader and protector of the Jewish people.

Consider two brick masons. The first was asked, "What are you doing?" He replied, "I am laying brick. Can't you see, dummy?" The second worker was asked, "What are you doing?" He replied, "I am building a skyscraper." There is a difference between just doing something and having something to do. Without a clear focus and purpose, we lose our sense of being. Samson got distracted from his divine purpose due to this very reason.

In Judges 14:5-14, Samson is at it again, wading into the pool of disobedience. A wild animal attacks Samson in a vineyard. What, for goodness' sake, is a Nazarite doing in a vineyard? Is he there to get grapes to make wine? He was to stay away from strong drinks, and here he is, plain as day, in the wrong place at the wrong time. You talk about temptation; Samson was playing with fire.

On his way home, Samson saw that the bees made honey in the carcass of the lion he had recently killed. He scooped up the honey and ate. And not only did he eat, but he brought his parents a portion. Sadly, they were unaware of just where the honey came from. Now, they were defiled. **(Num 19:11-13)** Samson had deceived his parents, and he would later, down the road, be deceived as well by his women. We reap what we sow. **(Gal 6:7)**

In Eastern religions, as we know, the parents choose the bride for the son as a tradition. On the contrary, Samson made this decision for himself, not his parents. This choice of Samson started the domino effect, and everything began to go sideways. Samson wanted what he wanted. And boy, did he get it. It led to sin, heartache, and embarrassment for himself and his family.

His mom and dad should have said no to their only spoiled son's marriage and put their foot down. I am an only child, so I know exactly how the family conversation led to this. His parents were trying to please him and keep peace in the house simultaneously. But in the process, they displeased God.

Samson won the battle but lost the war. The wedding was on, and they went to Timnah to arrange and consummate the marriage.

Samson put forth a riddle at the wedding party, and the girl got Samson to unravel the puzzle because her hometown goons threatened her. If she did not get the answer to the riddle, her family would be killed. The riddle was so captivating and filled with intrigue. **Judges 14:14** records the riddle, "And he said unto them, out of the eater came forth meat, and out of the strong came forth sweetness. And they could not in three days expound the riddle."

If the Philistines got the riddle correct, 30 of them would get a suit of clothes. If they failed to get the riddle correct, they would owe Samson 30 suits of clothes. This was where the trouble began, and things got interesting indeed. The Philistines did what they could to gain an edge and win, and they were going to squeeze Samson's girlfriend for all they could get out of her to solve the riddle.

Riddles were commonplace in antiquity and were what teachers call critical thinking today. It was a puzzle. It was a mental gymnastics exercise to test one's wits and reasoning capacity. It was antithetical because Samson's life was a puzzle, and he had to wait to see how each piece of his episodes came together to create a canvas of chaos.

So, this woman was under pressure from the fellows in town, who wanted to cash in big on-the-door prizes, 30 suits of clothes. They had tried for three days and came up empty-handed in their brainstorming. They had no intention of playing the game fairly; they wanted to cheat. So, they asked Samson's girlfriend to commit espionage for them. Out of fear, she gave in and sweet-talked Samson with crocodile tears for several days, and the Philistines got the answer to the riddle and won the prizes. They got the winning trophies of clothes. When Samson discovered his girlfriend had dumped him, he angrily went to Ashkelon and killed thirty men. In frustration, he then stripped them of their clothes and gave dead men's clothes to the Philistines as their consolation prize for getting the riddle answer correct.

Samson returned home defeated, betrayed, and embarrassed; Samson's unstable and violent side was at last revealed. Furthermore, he left, abandoned his bride to his best man, and stole gifts off dead men's backs. Here was a judge who knew how to dish out justice. His riddle was his poetic justice. It was his and not God's.

In addition (Judges 15), to make the wedding riddle story even more sinister, the Bible says, "Samson's wife was given by her father to his best man who was in the wedding party at the feast." When Samson went to visit his wife (Obviously, he remained in Israel, and she remained with the Philistines even after their wedding), her father-in-law informed him that he had given her in marriage to somebody else because he assumed Samson was disappointed in her actions of betrayal and did not want her anymore as a bride.

Judges 15:2 says, "I truly thought you must hate her," her father explained, "so I gave her in marriage to your best man. But look, her younger sister is even more beautiful than she is. Marry her instead."

Moreover, the father tried to smooth things over and convince Samson to take her younger sister instead. He even threw Samson's chosen wife under the bus by saying her sister is better-looking anyway! "Isn't she the better pick?" Take her instead. Talk about drama. Good grief and good night, Irene.

Samson got so upset over this marriage mess that he ran out and caught 300 foxes, tied their tails together in pairs, tied burning torches to their tails, and set them free to run like a bat out of hell in the Philistine's fields. They burned down everything in their path, including vineyards and olive groves. Sirens went off, and the fire department of that day really had a tough time putting out the fire. Here it is again, Samson's violent behavior, temper, and minimal self-control front and center. The fire of anger raging inside was now out of control on the outside. The whole world saw it, and it was not a pretty sight.

This biblical account shows meddling kinfolk and neighbors wanting to run the marriage before it starts. Some kinfolks are just tattletales and love to start a mess. They tell lies about what they heard or what somebody told them and feed it to the bride or the groom, and it creates division, and that is what they want, especially when the in-laws are really outlaws. Rivalry in families is dangerous because they are out to destroy the union. Not everybody in the family will always approve of the marriage. They will sow discord and make it seem like this union is a bad choice. It seems that girlfriend #1 had some good outside help to set up the spirit of distrust between them.

Meddling and the spread of rumors are extensive on social media today. Someone sees your man or gal out talking with somebody else, snaps a picture, sends it to their phone, or makes a post. This is where all hell breaks loose. If you cannot know the context in which the picture was snapped, how in the world do you really know what is going on? The whole idea is to create enough doubt in your mind and let your imagination run wild. If you play by the world's rules, you will suffer a loss every time; I guarantee it.

Mind you, people can get many things wrong. You don't always see what you think you saw. Let me explain a real-life incident. I went into a convenience store that I visit regularly, and since I am a public figure, people just know me. I don't know them, but they know me. I went into the store to get some items after I had pumped my gas. My wife, Carol, came into the store later, behind me. Little did I know the clerk in the store knew me, but I did not know her. She's a noisy Rosie, I knew that, and she never spoke to me. Carol came in later and started talking to me. Carol had a different hairdo than she normally wears, and the clerk in question did not recognize Carol with the new hairstyle. When Carol started talking, she recognized Carol's voice. She hollered and said, "Carol, that's you! I thought the preacher had brought another woman in here!"

Now, you see how stuff gets started. We don't see what we think we see all the time. The Philistines pushed their way into the courtship, ruining everything using deception. This lesson teaches us to be mindful of family and friends reading more into something than what is actually there. Had the Philistines guys played fair, things might have turned out differently.

Now, Jewish rabbis claim this was an honorable marriage in the making. Many marriages start with good intentions, but sometimes the ceremony is canceled. I witnessed a wedding where the groom was so intoxicated over the fear of getting married that after the wedding, he told his bride he was going to the store and left the reception. He never came back! Like Samson, everything stopped before it ever got started. Thus, the relationship with girlfriend #1 ends- based solely on love at first sight.

Love, at first sight, can be electric but also suffers a power shortage. A sudden connection can be real, but it needs to be tested at all levels of the dating ritual and romance. Let's look at **girlfriend #2.**

Chapter Three

Samson's Girlfriend #2

The Prostitute

"Wet paint, don't touch," that's what the sign says, but if you come back a few hours later, you will certainly find handprints. It's just human nature to do what you are told not to do. Men seem to gravitate toward doing what they cannot have or doing what is prohibited. Samson was no exception.

The call girl Samson met this time and had a sexual encounter with was a common hustler. The more expensive ones did not do business out of a house but rather camped out near the city gate with their faces covered. Furthermore, I am convinced that the call girl in question was a Philistine government informant. The manner of her business and the tourists and traders that stopped by gave her an edge on the information. Later on, we will see her superiors coming to her for information on her recent patron that put her newfound boyfriend, Samson, at risk.

Samson's life so far didn't look too great, but he was included in the Hall of Fame. **(Heb 11:32)** In Judges 16:1-3, Samson was at it again, a bite at the same apple, a Philistine woman. This time, it was a streetwalker, a prostitute.

Prostitution is still a health hazard today. We can thank Columbus and his crew for bringing a variety of diseases to these American shores in the great Columbian Exchange. Men are aware of the dangers of prostitution, but the thrill and pleasure of its lewdness, for some, overrides the health dangers that come along with it.

Prostitution is believed to be one of the world's oldest professions. Its practice can be traced back to ancient times, even to this present age of licensed houses in Las Vegas. Senator Harry Reid tried to ban them, but it proved too much of an elicit fun enterprise and too lucrative to abandon and make illegal.

Prostitution has always been a public health concern. Research has shown that women and men who engage in such activities were exposed to abuse, violence, abandonment, drugs, and a life of poverty. It is a life that reveals the brokenness of one's esteem. There are at least seven tools, according to scripture, that a prostitute has in her toolbox that she uses to work her magic on a man. These spells and potions did a number on Samson. Consider:

1. She flatters with her lips. **Proverbs 2:16** "To deliver thee from the strange woman, *even* from the stranger *which* flattereth with her words."

2. She pays no attention to her home training and refuses to follow her parents' sound teachings. **Proverbs 2:17** "Which forsaketh the guide of her youth, and forgetteth the covenant of her God."

3. She is in business to destroy men's lives. **Proverbs 2:19:** "None who go to her return, nor do they regain the paths of life."

4. She lives in the red-light district, which makes for a short life, but she does it anyway. **Proverbs 2:18:** "Entering her house leads to death; it is the road to the grave."

5. She comes at a cheap price, even as a loaf of bread, and as somebody else's woman, she is prey on your life. **Proverbs 6:26** "For the price of a prostitute is only a loaf of bread, but a married woman hunts down a precious life."

6. She is the cause of others going to hell. **Proverbs 5:5** "Her feet go down to death; her steps lead straight to the grave."

7. She destroys men permanently to the point of no repair. **Proverbs 6:32** "But whoso committeth adultery with a woman lacketh understanding he that doeth it destroyeth his own soul."

No one starts out in life with this sexual enterprise in their mind as a career. It becomes a last resort for survival. We generally associate this profession with women, but to a smaller degree, men also peddle these notions.

The church where I serve as a pastor is right in the heart of what the old folks called the "Red Light District," Nelson Street. Occasionally, these street walkers come to church, and we reach out to them and do what we can to show them love and Jesus. The problem with steering them away from a life of prostitution comes from their lack of education, employability skills, housing, and not having a consistent address. If people who find themselves in this situation are ever to break this sordid lifestyle, our communities and the church must take the initiative to provide resources for a better life. Love and the will to do something is the answer.

America is the richest nation on earth, and we do not show enough genuine concern for the least, the lonely, and the left out. Sadly, even our veterans are treated as second-class citizens, and many are homeless.

The Bible says, "***Then Samson went to Gaza.***" Gaza was a Philistine city located near the Mediterranean Sea. It was situated on the main road that allowed travel between Egypt, Babylon, and Assyria. It was a commercial powerhouse and a military station and outpost. The name "***Gaza***" means "***strength,***" and it was a Philistine stronghold. It was a place known for its wickedness as well as idolatry. It was not a good place for a man of such stature as Samson, the judge of Israel, to be a sightseeing tourist.

Today, there is little evidence of the glories of Gaza's past. Excavations reveal only traces of sand dunes. Joshua and the Israelites were never able to conquer Gaza, so the Philistines remained a constant thorn to the Israelites. (Josh.10:41, 11:22)

It really does matter where you spend most of your time. Samson found himself in Gaza, in enemy territory, courting and looking for romance as usual. You can be certain that if you consistently find yourself in places surrounded by sinful activity or even in a place where you can be tempted to sin, you are setting yourself up for trouble big time. The Bible warns us to avoid places where we might be tempted to sin. **Proverbs 4:14-15** says, *"Enter not into the path of the wicked, and go not in the way of evil men. Avoid it, pass not by it, turn from it, and pass away."*

Let me share a story concerning a billionaire heiress who had purchased a brand-new Bentley Flying Spur and was looking for a professional driver. She advertised in the local paper and received several good prospects. She had all of them come to her mansion at the same time and look over the fine motorcar and get a feel for it. She interviewed them individually and chose four of the best applicants out of the pool. She asked prospect number 1, "If you could drive up to that wall over by the fence, how close could you get to it without scratching my Bentley?" He said, "About maybe a foot," the second said, "About 4 inches," the third one said, "About 6 or 7 inches, 8 inches at the most." The fourth prospect said he really did not know how close he could get to the wall without damaging the car. He looked a bit shaken, knowing how expensive the fine hand-built motorcar was. He told the heiress, "I would try to stay as far away from the wall as possible." He understood that true skill is simply the ability to avoid trouble, not get as close to it as possible. Samson never used the skill of staying away from trouble. He always drove right up to it.

Chapter Four

Delilah's Sleeping Beauty Salon

In Judges 16:4-6, the drama continues to unfold, and we find Samson is again back in enemy territory. It just doesn't get any better. He is there not to fight, but he is there to have fun. This last visit to Gaza ultimately brings Samson's judgeship to an end. Samson will never see his mother or his father again after he meets the wrong lady; her name is Delilah. She is girlfriend #3.

All the women that came to Samson were Philistine women with questionable characters. In no way did they complement him in his leadership role in the economy of the Nation of Israel.

So, we have seen this movie before and know the outcome if you are like most critical-thinking people. Why do good men chase the wrong women? Good question, right? Men love to hunt; he is on the hunt whenever we see Samson. He is looking for something even if it's wrong, wrong, wrong. Men are hunters and love the chase to catch something or someone. Women are receivers. Delilah is a professional. She has been at her craft for a long time. This woman is polished and more sophisticated than the rest, which explains how she could reel in such a big fish in the person of Samson. She is smooth and slick as butter. She is dangerous and a gold digger. She is all about the Benjamins!

Delilah was a Philistine woman from the Valley of Sorek. Her name means "the longing and dainty one." She was also an informant or a spy for the Philistines. The patrons that came to town gave her access to information that would prove helpful to the rulers of the people.

35

In Gaza, the word got around that Samson was sleeping with Delilah. The rulers came to her to offer her a bribe. They make her an offer she cannot refuse.

When the Lords of the Philistines found out that she was sleeping with the enemy, this was their chance to swoop in and go for the kill. They made a deal with Delilah, a shakedown to get the secret to Samson's powerful strength. **(Judges 16:5-6)** And the lords of the Philistines came up to her and said to her, "Entice him, and find out where his great strength *lies,* and by what *means* we may overpower him, that we may bind him to afflict him; and every one of us will give you eleven hundred *pieces* of silver."

Now, the offer is that the Lords would offer her 1,100 pieces of silver a part. To get the secret was a great deal of money. This was life-changing and would have set her up for life. Judges 3:3 says that there were five Lords of the Philistines. They would be equal to the mob bosses of their day. According to the computation of silver's value, she was paid a little over $86,000. The value of her bribe would be in today's money would approach over $700,000. The word "entice" in verse 5 is an act to lure someone to become entrapped, gullible, simple, or silly. In plain English, Samson was played like a cheap violin.

The Bible says Samson was in love with Delilah, but she was never in love with him. This one-sided relationship is all too often the landscape in life. It is very hurtful when you give one hundred percent and your mate contributes zero. Some people get into relationships for various reasons, and it's not always love. It can be security; it can be status. They like sex, access to money, political power, or a way to get out of the house. Whatever the reason, it should always be about real love and respect.

As the story goes, a little boy was lost in a huge department store in Atlanta during the height of the Christmas season. He was overwhelmed by the size of the crowd, the store, and the tremendous store merchandise that filled the shelves. He got distracted and did not notice that his dear mother was no longer standing near him, so he started crying uncontrollably. The customers came by and started to calm him down by giving him money and shouting Merry Christmas. $5, $10, and $3, and a whopping $20 were constantly being placed in his hands. The manager had been watching the whole scene on camera and came to the little boy and told him, "I know where your mother is. Stop crying. Let me go get her". The little boy said, "I know where she is too. Now be quiet and get away from me." We know when we are doing wrong, but it's what we get out of it that motivates us to keep doing it. Samson has a bad case of the can't help it.

Delilah certainly knew that her actions were not honorable. She did not care; all she was concerned about was what she was getting out of the deal. It was MONEY. She used the weakness of Samson to get what she wanted. It is called deception. The spirit of deception keeps showing up in Samson's life. He deceives and is being deceived himself.

All couples in love and romance should take the blindfolders off and look at the warning signs on the dashboard of their mind. Samson had no excuse. He saw all the warning signs and refused to accept the reality of a wrong end. I believe life is too short to spend time going nowhere fast. The power of love is so sweeping and can easily cloud our thinking.

I brought a girl home in my early days of courtship. I thought, man oh man, she is the one as she was pretty, intelligent, highly educated, and religious. I asked my mother what she thought about the girl; momma said, "She is a fool." I said, "Awe, momma, don't say that." But sure enough, it was not long before I discovered that she was undoubtedly right, a fool! Those who love us the most can see what we cannot see. It is called discernment. Consider their advice if you have people around you; they honestly see what you cannot see. It is invaluable indeed.

Moreover, the looks of beauty, hips, lips, and perfume are not enough. A real God-fearing man must be moved not by the sensual but by the Spirit of the living God. I see Samson sitting on the porch with his head in Delilah's lap, thinking this is a slice of heaven, not realizing she is getting ready to give him an expensive haircut.

God-fearing marriages should bring people closer together to achieve their dreams and fulfill God's will for their lives. In Malachi 2:16, God says he hates divorce. It is easy to hook up with someone, but the breakup is not as easy, especially if the distribution of assets and children is involved. I know from pastoral experience that wrong relationships can cause unsuspecting partners to end up on drugs by inducement, low self-esteem, affiliation with opposing groups, and the total denunciation of one's relationship with the Lord as King. Be careful with your soul. It's the most valuable thing you have. (Matthew 16:26)

I never met a woman who did not love money and loved to shop. Most women seemed to have the same instructor regarding loving money and the material things money can provide. Nothing is wrong with having money, but it is wrong to let money have you.

According to a recent study by Spectrum Family Law, in March 2023, financial instability is the number one reason couples get divorced, followed by infidelity. The devil knew how to put the tremendous big *enchilada* on Samson's plate.

Today's New Age society dabbles in the use of crystals. They are believed to give off energy, calm fears, emotions, protect and emit positive energy. The Philistines were highly superstitious and had difficulty explaining Samson's enormous strength; therefore, in their fear of him, they resorted to extreme measures to find its source. Did he have an amulet? Was he some demi-god? They had to find out.

Shady women are still cashing in today. Camping outside the hotels where celebrities, stars, and ball players are rumored to stay, they will be able to catch them and entice them, get pregnant, and cash in on their fortunes. There is indeed nothing new under the sun.

Ecclesiastes 1:9 (That which has been what will be, that which *is* done is what will be done, and *there is* nothing new under the sun).

Samson and Delilah's relationship was based solely on lies. Facebook allows you to be whoever you want to be. You can type anything in your profile, stage a scene, and everything looks real. Many people have gotten taken over under false pretense.

Samson lies about where he gets his strength. In verses 16:7-10 Samson says, "Bind me with seven green witts." Witts were the guts of animals and, when dried, were extremely strong. In verse 10, Delilah challenges Samson. Furthermore, in verses 13 and 14, Delilah says to Samson, "All this time you have been making a fool of me and lying to me. Tell me how you can be tied." He replied, "If you weave the seven braids of my head into the fabric on the loom and tighten it with the pin, I'll become as weak as any other man." Samson is dancing on the edge of brinkmanship.

Deception is the game that is played on Samson time and time again. Deception is a game also played on Isaac. In **Genesis 27,** Isaac is an older man. We will learn another rich lesson from him later in his young years that I will share later. Isaac is old and blind and about to give out the blessing, so he asks his son Esau to get some wild game and prepare it for him to eat. Isaac is about to bless Esau, the firstborn before he dies. Rebekah, his wife, overhears the conversation. Rebekah wants her "favorite son," Jacob, to get the blessing. In **Genesis 27:5-40** look how the deception unfolds.

[5] But Rebekah overheard what Isaac had said to his son Esau. So, when Esau left to hunt for the wild game, [6], she told her son, Jacob, "Listen. I overheard your father say to Esau, [7] 'Bring me some wild game and prepare me a delicious meal. Then I will bless you in the Lord's presence before I die.' [8] Now, my son, listen to me. Exactly do as I tell you. [9] Go out to the flocks and bring me two fine young goats. I'll use them to prepare your father's favorite dish. [10] Then take the food to your father so he can eat it and bless you before he dies."

[11] "But look," Jacob replied to Rebekah, "my brother, Esau, is a hairy man, and my skin is smooth. [12] What if my father touches me? He'll see that I'm trying to trick him, and then he'll curse me instead of blessing me."

[13] But his mother replied, "Then let the curse fall on me, my son! Just do what I tell you. Go out and get the goats for me!"

[14] So Jacob went out and got the young goats for his mother. Rebekah took them and prepared a delicious meal, just as Isaac liked it. [15] Then she took Esau's favorite clothes, which were there in the house, and gave them to her younger son, Jacob. [16] She covered his arms and the smooth part of his neck with the skin of the young goats. [17] Then she gave Jacob the delicious meal, including freshly baked bread.

[18] So Jacob took the food to his father. "My father?" he said.

"Yes, my son," Isaac answered. "Who are you—Esau or Jacob?"

[19] Jacob replied, "It's Esau, your firstborn son. I've done as you told me. Here is the wild game. Now sit up and eat it to give me your blessing."

[20] Isaac asked, "How did you find it so quickly, my son?"

"The Lord your God put it in my path!" Jacob replied.

[21] Then Isaac told Jacob, "Come closer so I can touch you and make sure that you are Esau." [22] So Jacob went closer to his father, and Isaac touched him. "The voice is Jacob's, but the hands are Esau's," Isaac said. [23] But he did not recognize Jacob because Jacob's hands felt hairy like Esau's. So Isaac prepared to bless Jacob. [24] "But are you my son Esau?" he asked.

"Yes, I am," Jacob replied.

[25] Then Isaac said, "Now, my son, bring me the wild game. Let me eat it, and then I will bless you." So, Jacob took the food to his father, and Isaac ate it. He also drank the wine that Jacob served him. [26] Then Isaac said to Jacob, "Please come a little closer and kiss me, my son."

27 So Jacob went over and kissed him. And when Isaac caught the smell of his clothes, he was finally convinced and blessed his son. He said, Ah! The smell of my son is like the smell of the outdoors, which the Lord has blessed!

28 "From heaven's dew and the earth's richness, may God always give you abundant harvests of grain and bountiful new wine. **29** May many nations become your servants, and may they bow down to you. May you be the master over your brothers, and may your mother's sons bow down to you. All who curse you will be cursed, and all who bless you will be blessed."

30 As soon as Isaac had finished blessing Jacob, and almost before Jacob had left his father, Esau returned from his hunt. **31** Esau prepared a delicious meal and brought it to his father. Then he said, "Sit up, my father, and eat my wild game so you can give me your blessing."

32 But Isaac asked him, "Who are you?"

Esau replied, "It's your firstborn son, Esau."

33 Isaac began to tremble uncontrollably and said, "Then who just served me wild game? I have already eaten it and blessed him just before you came. And yes, that blessing must stand!"

34 When Esau heard his father's words, he cried loudly and bitterly. "Oh, my father, what about me? Bless me, too!" he begged.

35 But Isaac said, "Your brother was here, and he tricked me. He has taken away your blessing."

36 Esau exclaimed, "No wonder his name is Jacob; for now, he has cheated me twice. He took my rights as the firstborn, and now he has stolen my blessing. Oh, haven't you saved even one blessing for me?"

37 Isaac said to Esau, "I have made Jacob your master and have declared that all his brothers will be his servants. I have guaranteed him an abundance of grain and wine—what is left for me to give you, my son?"

[38] Esau pleaded, "But do you have only one blessing? Oh, my father, bless me, too!" Then Esau broke down and wept.

[39] Finally, his father, Isaac, said to him,

"You will live away from the richness of the earth and away from the dew of the heaven above.[40] You will live by your sword and serve your brother. But when you decide to break free, you will shake his yoke from your neck."

Jacob and his mother, Rebekah, entered a conspiracy to deceive, which worked but separated the family. Jacob had to run to keep his brother Esau from killing him. Little does he know that Jacob will never see his parents again.

Jacob went through several life-changing events filled with deceit and being cheated out of his money and dignity. This same spirit of deception continued to haunt him and his entire household. He succeeded in getting his brother to sell his birthright for a bowl of soup. Jacob got what he wanted but lived as a fugitive for the rest of his life.

It's a long narrative, but I just wanted to show that people are just people regardless of the times. Some people will go to any extent to achieve their desired ends, even if it is deceptive, evil, and unrighteous.

Delilah uses the same playbook, a different version of deception, but deception nonetheless. This act of trickery is repeated throughout the Bible. Delilah is the smoothest of operators of the Philistine women.

Nevertheless, Delilah used the same as Timnah's girlfriend: "If you love me, you will." In Chapter 16 verse 15-16, she says, "Then she said to him, "How can you say, 'I love you,' when your heart *is* not with me? You have mocked me these three times and have not told me where your great strength *lies*." Delilah nagged Samson until she wore him down to a frazzle. He gave in and told her the secret to his strength. It was her fake tears, the tone of her voice, the gestures of her hands that were a lullaby that rocked him to sleep. She got him good. She begins to cut his hair. He falls fast to sleep. My dad always told me, "Son, if you play around with trash, it will get in your eyes."

I never would let my wife Carol cut my son Simeon's hair as a little boy; I was so hell-bent on believing Simeon would end up like Samson, deceived! Because of my superstitions, I would never let my wife cut my son's hair. Whenever I caught her doing it, I would shout and take the clippers. Due to my beliefs, it also took me a long time to let a lady barber cut my hair. I never saw my daddy let a woman cut his hair, and the barber shop we went to had a lady barber always on duty.

Well, time brings about a change. I must confess that the lady barber who cut my hair was BJ. It so happened that one Saturday morning, I was pushed for time. The barber shop was full; the fellas were shooting off their lies and joking as usual. There is nothing like a barbershop; it's a hotbed for gossip. So, I needed to be at a service at 11 o'clock, about 40 miles away. Well, BJ was the owner of the Barber and Beauty Salon. Her chair was the only chair free, and she was sitting in the chair reading the local newspaper to pass the time. Okay, here I go. Reluctantly, I asked her can you cut my hair? She said sure, preacher, I took the chair, and her touch was amazingly soft and relaxing. It was a smooth cut and silky, unlike the rough hands of a man's cut. To top it off, she gave me a complimentary shave. The hot soap and hot towel wrap were something to feel and experience. I am too embarrassed to confess that I went fast to sleep like Samson. So, I understand what Samson was up against in Delilah's Salon. The soft touch and her soothing voice rocked him to sleep.

So then, Delilah goes in for the kill and is about to get paid. She cuts seven locks of hair from Samson's head while he sleeps physically and spiritually. Seven in scripture represents completion.

Let us note:

The Lord's Prayer has seven petitions.

The world was completed in six days, and on the seventh day, God rested.

There are seven notes on a musical scale.

There are seven holes in your head.

There are seven days in the week.

On the cross, Jesus spoke seven times

There are seven continents in the world.

Seven is the number of completion, and the end of Samson is drawing near. The Bible says he "wist not," which means he did not realize the awful fate he would soon endure. (V.20) Sin robbed him of all his powers as a judge of Israel. Delilah had nothing to lose because she never boasted of anything of significant value. She had nothing to lose and everything to gain, but in all the things she lost, she lost her soul as well.

In his weakness, Samson is mocked and seized by the Philistines and hauled off to the temple of Dagon as a prisoner of war. The mighty has finally fallen all because he is in the wrong place at the wrong time. He is not in Gaza to fight as a man of power, but he is in Gaza on a rendezvous for sexual pleasure and romance.

There are at least seven reasons why a man should stay away from a prostitute who works the red-light district recorded in scripture:

Consider:

1. She is highly deceptive **Proverbs 5:3** "For the lips of a strange woman drop *as* a honeycomb, and her mouth *is* smoother than oil."

2. She will bring you to a bitter and lousy end. **Proverbs 5:4** "But her end is bitter as wormwood, sharp as a two-edged sword."

3. She will reduce you to a loaf of bread. **Proverbs 6:26** "For a prostitute can be had for a loaf of bread, but another man's wife preys on your very life."

4. She will ruin your body and health. **Proverbs 5:11** "And thou mourn at last when thy flesh and thy body are consumed."

5. She is unstable and unpredictable. **Proverbs 5:6 NIV** "She gives no thought to the way of life; her paths wander, but she does not know it."

6. She will destroy your reputation **Proverbs 5:9 NIV** "lest you lose your honor to others and your dignity to one who is cruel."

7. She will take your money and steal your wealth from you.

Proverbs 5:10 NLT "Strangers will consume your wealth, and someone else will enjoy the fruit of your labor."

In the house of Dagon, Samson is about to bring the house down as his final act as judge, as the sun is setting in his life. A lad leads Samson, who has had his eyes gouged out as a child, helpless and defenseless. That is paradoxical, the so-called strong and manly being led by an adolescent. Once a man, twice a child.

However, Samson does a beautiful act amid his predicament; he prays to God for his strength to return. Samson's hair was shaved all off, which was an even greater humiliation for a man of his status.

I attended Gentry High School and received a full band scholarship to attend Mississippi Valley State University under the direction of Leonard Tramiel. He was a tough, non-sense director. As a freshman, the first order of business upon hitting the campus for the two-week band camp was that every male band member had to have all their hair cut down to a ball. It was the initiation phase, and the girls had to wear toilet paper in their hair as ribbons for the probation period as well. I can sympathize with Samson's hair being cut off. It is a humbling experience.

I can feel him crying as they shaved his head. Delilah cut seven locks from his head, but to add insult to injury, the Philistines shaved his hair. The unfolding narrative of Samson says that he prayed, and the Lord remembered him. As sinful as Samson was, God was still gracious and recognized him. Samson prayed. The Bible recorded his prayer, but he prayed mentally, and who knows what he and the Lord talked about.

Judges 16:28 Then Samson prayed to the LORD, **"Sovereign LORD, remember me again. O God, please strengthen me just one more time. With one blow, let me pay back the Philistines for losing my two eyes."** I am sure that prayer is always in order, and in the spot, Samson found himself. Let us give credit where credit is due. God answered his prayer.

Blind, bound, and bewildered, he prays to God that his strength and as his hair begins to grow again. **(Judges 16:22)** The Philistines poke fun and make sport of him. The Philistines believe their God had delivered Samson into their hands as he threads out a grinding mill.

In the height of their drunken stupor, blind Samson asked that his hands be placed on the two large columns, and he pushed the building down. He kills three thousand men and women. In his death, he killed more than he killed in his lifetime. He was willing to die for his people and rid them of some of their enemies. It was the last thing he could do, and he did a fantastic job. Thus, it ends the life of Samson the Hercules of Israel. Samson is the last!

Samson and Solomon were the most muscular and wisest, as recorded in the Bible. They were both conquered by women. Ironically, both luminaries' names start with an **"s"** and end with an **"n."** Solomon made a powerful confession worth noting in **Ecclesiastes 7:26** "And I find more bitter than death the woman, whose heart is snares and nets, and her hands as bands: whoso pleaseth God shall escape from her; but she shall take the sinner."

Samson ruled for 20 years. But 40 years is ascribed to him because, after his death, the Philistines became fearful of the Jewish people and left them alone for some reason.

Chapter Five

The Undercover Agent: The Jezebel Spirit

I am convinced that Samson was influenced by some type of spirit other than the Holy Spirit because his behavior clearly shows that he was being controlled by some force that caused him to be driven by evil and lust and not righteousness constantly.

The spirit that manifests in his life points to the Jezebel Spirit. The charismatic movement coined this term, but it is credible when explaining Samson and his repetitive choice of women.

Historically, Jezebel was a wicked Phoenician Queen responsible for the fashionable style of painting her eyelids and wearing makeup. The cosmetics industry can thank her for her originality. The cosmetic industry boasts today of earning over 49 billion dollars in 2022, according to **Statista**. Jezebel's preferred fashion of painting her eyelids is still in vogue to this very day. Women the world over continue in this tradition as we speak.

In **2 Kings 9:30,** it says, "Then Jehu went to Jezreel. When Jezebel heard about it, she put on eye makeup, arranged her hair, and looked out of a window." Jezebel was known for her fashion and her hairstyles as well. Jezebel epitomizes using fashion and style to grab attention and wheel and deal. She was the wife of King Ahab, who ruled Israel for 20 years and was a terrible king of the Northern Kingdom. His downfall was due to his marriage to Jezebel. He was king on the throne, but Jezebel was the power behind the throne. Ahab was a puppet, a weak, henpecked man who wanted the title of king and did not mind being controlled and manipulated by his overly aggressive and dominating wife.

Jezebel was the promoter of Baal worship; she even had false prophets. During this time, the people of God were torn between two opinions. They were unsure who to pledge their allegiance to. Was Yahweh the supreme deity, or was it Baal? It would take a contest on Mount Carmel to settle the case.

1 Kings 18:21 says, Elijah went before the people and said, "How long will you waver between two opinions? If the LORD is God, follow him; but if Baal is God, follow him. But the people said nothing."

Jezebel had a hatred for Elijah and killed many of God's prophets, and after the contest on Mount Carmel where God showed himself superior to the God of Baal by raining down fire on the sacrifice, Elijah went and hid in a cave out of fear for his life.

1 Kings 19:9-14 "Then he came to a cave and lodged there; behold, the word of the LORD *came* to him, and He said to him, What are you doing here, Elijah? He said, I have been very zealous for the LORD, the God of hosts; for the sons of Israel have forsaken Your covenant, torn down Your altars, and killed Your prophets with the sword. And I alone am left; they seek my life, to take it away."

So, He said, "Go forth and stand on the mountain before the LORD." And behold, the LORD was passing by! And a great and strong wind was rending the mountains and breaking in pieces the rocks before the LORD, *but* the LORD *was* not in the wind. And after the wind an earthquake, *but* the LORD *was* not in the earthquake. After the earthquake, there was a fire, *but* the LORD *was* not in the fire and a sound of a gentle blowing after the fire. When Elijah heard *it,* he wrapped his face in his mantle and went out and stood at the entrance of the cave. And behold, a voice *came* to him and said, "What are you doing here, Elijah?" Then he said, "I have been very zealous for the

LORD, the God of hosts; for the sons of Israel have forsaken Your covenant, torn down Your altars, and killed Your prophets with the sword. And I alone am left; they seek my life, to take it away."

God came and asked him, "What are you doing here?". After God had this business meeting with Elijah, he was filled with renewed faith to go to the end.

When we look at the colossal threads of seduction that Samson's women spin, we can see the spirit of Jezebel at work. This spirit does not just manifest itself in women, but it also manifests itself in men. Their goals are the same: control, control, control. This spirit has broken up churches, marriages, corporations, politicians' careers, and the nation's leadership.

This spirit is driven by the enormous three: power, sex, and financial gain, to mention a few. All three were active in the women that Samson encountered. Most especially Delilah.

Moreover, this spirit loves to have its way no matter the cost, even if it takes murder to achieve the desired end. In **1 Kings 21:1-16,** it says, **"**Now it came about after these things that Naboth the Jezreelite had a vineyard which *was* in Jezreel beside the palace of Ahab, king of Samaria. Ahab spoke to Naboth, saying, Give me your vineyard, that I may have it for a vegetable garden because it is close beside my house, and I will give you a better vineyard than it in its place; if you like, I will give you the price of it in money." But Naboth told Ahab, "The LORD forbid me that I should give you the inheritance of my fathers." So Ahab came into his house sullen and vexed because of Naboth the Jezreelite)s word, for he said, "I will not give you the inheritance of my fathers." And he lay down on his bed, turned away his face, and ate no food.

But Jezebel, his wife, came to him and said to him, "How is it that your spirit is so sullen that you are not eating food?" So he said to her, "Because I spoke to Naboth the Jezreelite and said to him, give me your vineyard for money; or else, if it pleases you, I will give you a vineyard in its place. But he said I would not give you my vineyard." Jezebel, his wife, said, "Do you now reign over Israel? Arise, eat bread, and let your heart be joyful; I will give you the vineyard of Naboth the Jezreelite."

So, she wrote letters in Ahab's name, sealed them with his seal, and sent letters to the elders and the nobles living with Naboth in his city. She wrote in the letters, saying, "Proclaim a fast and seat Naboth at the head of the people, and seat two worthless men before him, and let them testify against him, saying, 'You cursed God and the king.' Then take him out and stone him to death."

So the men of his city, the elders, and the nobles who lived in his city did as Jezebel had sent *word* to them, just as it was written in the letters she had sent them. They proclaimed a fast and seated Naboth at the head of the people. Then the two worthless men came in and sat before him, and the helpless men testified against him, even against Naboth, before the people, saying, "Naboth cursed God and the king." So, they took him outside the city and stoned him to death with stones. Then they sent *word* to Jezebel, saying, "Naboth has been stoned and is dead."

When Jezebel heard that Naboth had been stoned and was dead, Jezebel said to Ahab, "Arise, take possession of the vineyard of Naboth, the Jezreelite, which he refused to give you for money, for Naboth is not alive, but dead." When Ahab heard that Naboth was dead, Ahab arose to go down to the vineyard of Naboth the Jezreelite to take possession of it.

The spirit of Jezebel cares about nothing but what she wants and has an intense hatred for holy men who are out to do what is right and challenge her for her evil doings. The spirit of Jezebel will traffic in forgery. Jezebel forged her husband's signature on documents to have Naboth killed. This same spirit will also cause wives and husbands to forge signatures on checks, drain bank accounts, and steal passwords and pins to gain access to their spouses' or mates' financials. This spirit is dangerous, and a professional in sweet talking their way into your heart only to break it. Samson was mesmerized by it and deceived by it.

In **Matthew 14:1-11,** you can see this spirit strutting her stuff at a birthday party where Herod Antipas, in his drunken stupor, proposed that he would give his stepdaughter practically anything she wanted if she asked. Not knowing what to ask, she asked her mother and was told to ask for the head of John the Baptist. The daughter of Herodias danced a gig and did the twist for the preacher's head. This was the spirit of Jezebel at work, out to attack authority. John the Baptist had spoken against her marriage to Herod. Herod was scolded by John the Baptist for taking his brother's wife.

Jezebel hates authority, especially men in authority. If his leadership poses no threat to her program, she is fine. But the minute she is threatened and called out for her sinfulness, the gloves come off, and the fight is on.

Moreover, Jezebel is mentioned in Revelation as an active evil spirit at work in the end times. (**Revelation 2:18-29)** Every man must guard his soul because of her manipulative grip on relationships. John Paul Jackson, in his book "**Unmasking the Jezebel Spirt**" makes a very prophetic statement worth noting:

"A Jezebel spirit will influence a woman to criticize and belittle her husband, telling him he's not spiritual enough, bold enough, making enough money, or holding back from God's ministry waiting for her. She may apply subtle, manipulative pressure on him by simply sighing and commenting on how nice it would be to have this or that, knowing they can't afford it. She may also imply that if he loved her, he would work harder to provide for all her needs and desires.

Such manipulative ploys put incredible pressure on a man and increased his resentment. It may also cause him to flee into the arms of another woman who is more sensitive to his needs and makes him feel appreciated and thriving as a husband."

The spirit of Jezebel seeks to usurp authority and turn it on its head, and this was the whole modus operandi of Jezebel to manipulate the effectiveness and outcome of Samson's leadership all to her benefit. The only way to escape this influence is by the guidance of the Holy Spirit, a constant prayer life, exercising the power of binding and losing in Jesus' Name, and putting on the Whole Armor of God.

(**Ephesians 6:11-18**) "Put on the whole armor of God, that ye may be able to stand against the devil's wiles.

[12] For we wrestle not against flesh and blood, but against principalities, against powers, against the rulers of the darkness of this world, against spiritual wickedness in high places.

[13] Wherefore take unto you the whole armor of God, that ye may be able to withstand in the evil day, and having done all, to stand.

[14] Stand, therefore, having your loins girt about with truth, and having on the breastplate of righteousness.

[15] And your feet shod with the preparation of the gospel of peace;

[16] Above all, taking the shield of faith, wherewith ye shall be able to quench all the fiery darts of the wicked.

[17] And take the helmet of salvation, and the sword of the Spirit, which is the word of God:

[18] Praying always with all prayer and supplication in the Spirit and watching thereunto with all perseverance and supplication for all saints."

God doesn't like ugly; judgment comes to Jezebel's house after she flees in hiding. Having lost to the contest on Mt Carmel, she is seen looking out a window, trying to determine her next move. Elijah confronted her for her wickedness for leading Israel astray. Jehu, the general who ascended and became King, rode triumphantly into the land of Jezreel and commanded that the eunuchs lay hold of Jezebel and throw her out of the window. Jezebel's body hit the ground, and she was killed on impact. The dogs ate her body. It has been said power corrupts, absolute power corrupts absolutely.

Chapter Six

The Autopsy of Samson and His Women

Samson and his women deserve an autopsy out of courtesy. We need to seek the underlying causes of their demise to get to the bottom of their demise. What killed them? An autopsy is done as a matter of forensics to determine the why, how, and when the death occurred. This information will assist an investigator in determining whether a crime has been committed or was it an accident or natural death. It also will determine if a disease may have contributed to the individual's death. The cause of death is a fundamental aspect of the criminal justice system, especially in the court of law. Let us perform a spiritual autopsy to determine their cause of death.

The death of Samson and his women can be categorized in a simple, straightforward manner; these would be the same categories that would cause our spiritual death as well. There are seven deadly sins. We shall examine five of them in the lives of Samson and his women: pride, envy, lust, anger, and greed.

Pride: Pride is the first cause of death. Proverbs 16:18 reads, "Pride goes before destruction and a haughty spirit before a fall." This first disease was undoubtedly the foundational problem of Samson. Prideful of his lofty position as a judge, super strength, and miraculous birth all affected his prideful attitude. There is nothing wrong with having a sense of pride in yourself. The problem arises when we feel our station in life places us in a parading position of being better than someone else. That is where the danger arises. Samson's vow was nonnegotiable. His lifelong desire should have been to please God and no one else. Instead, he sought to satisfy himself with his choice of women, wine, and arrogance. He was the Superman of his day. He knew that most women had heard about him and would jump for the chance to be on his arm; pride goeth before a fall. It is one building block that builds a house that will collapse. Pride is so intoxicating that it also brings down leaders of countries, athletes, politicians, preachers, and billionaires. Pride is the only disease known to man that makes everyone sick except the one who has it.

Satan had a high position in heaven, and he lost that position because of his prideful spirit. He was not satisfied with being the anointed cherub of God; instead, he wanted to be like the Most High God. **(Isaiah 14:13-14)** Satan was created as a beautiful angel with all kinds of precious stones. This got the best of his ego as well. He was the chief music director in heaven and was created with instruments built into his body. He was a walking jukebox of sorts. He had pipes and tambourines **(Ezekiel 28: 12-15)**. Satan wanted to place himself, the created, above the creator. That is sheer madness, for God said it won't happen. Therefore, he was cast out of heaven. The use of having a prideful attitude was used against Adam and Eve. It was Satan's *Modus Operandi*. They were misinformed that God was holding back on them and did not want them to eat off the tree because it would make them compete with God and be like God. They fell for it. They lost twice: they lost their beautiful estate in Eden, and they died spiritually separated from God.

We can credit Satan for injecting this negative spirit of pride into the world; since its introduction, men and women have been falling ever since. As a result of pride, Samson forgot his purpose. He started following the way of sin and all its influences rather than the way of righteousness. What should have happened is that humility should have been his mainstay instead of having a prideful attitude. **James 4:6** states, "God opposes the proud but gives grace to the humble."

We must remember that all we hope to be and have achieved is because of an all-loving God. God blesses us not because of us; he blesses us despite ourselves. His amazing grace allows us to enjoy His unmerited favor and the power of his love in our lives. Humility causes us to see ourselves honestly and accurately. We are nothing but dust, and our lives are a vapor. **James 4:14** says, "Whereas ye know not what shall be on the morrow. For what is your life? It is even a vapor that appears for a bit and then vanishes away."

Consider this story: The story is about two brothers who grew up on a farm. One went away to college, earned a law degree, and became a partner in a prominent law firm in the state capital. The other brother stayed on the family farm. One day, the lawyer came and visited his brother, the farmer. "Why don't you go out and make a name for yourself and hold your head high in the world like me?" The brother pointed and said, "See that wheat field over there? Look closely. Only the empty heads stand up. Those that are well filled always bow low." Said differently, "The branch that bears the most fruit is bent the lowest to the ground." The way up is down! God's best gifts are not on the top shelf. They are on the bottom. We must bend and bow to reach greatness.

Moreover, Jesus spoke earnestly about humility in **Matthew 23: 11-12;** "But he that is greatest among you shall be your servant.[12] Whosoever shall exalt himself shall be abased, and he that shall humble himself shall be exalted." Also, in Philippians 2:6-7 Jesus' greatest expression of humility was when Jesus became what he was not yet without ceasing to be what he already was. God became a man. This was a wonderful display of humility to the very point of death!

Envy: The second cause of death was envy. The Philistines despised the Israelites because of their favor with Yahweh; therefore, they constantly hindered their peace and security. The women who were fond of Samson were used as pawns to get what their superiors wanted, and that was Samson.

Rick Warren makes a fascinating point about envy. He points out four damaging effects of envy. **(1)** Envy denies our uniqueness **(2)** Envy divides our attention **(3)** Envy uses up your time and energy**(4)** Envy leads to every other sin.

You may ask, what is an excellent working definition of envy? Consider this: Envy is defined by Merriam-Webster as the "painful or resentful awareness of an advantage enjoyed by another joined with a desire to possess the same advantage." This is precisely how the Philistines felt; they could not explain how Samson had so much supernatural strength and stamina. The Philistines were terrified of Samson's abilities, and they knew God had chosen him to protect Israel and that he was the buffer zone between them and Israel. Samson had the upper hand, and before they sought to take him on, they wanted to find the source of his power and learn how to disarm him. Whenever a police officer is confronted with a person with a weapon, the first order of business is to disarm the suspect. That is where Samson's girlfriend comes into play. Samson's girlfriend would be the secret agent who would assist them in their discovery of Samson's power and how to disarm him.

Envy is a vice that shows up all through the Bible. Especially in the life of Joseph, envy got him thrown in a pit and sold to Potiphar. In addition, we can see it in the life of King Saul and his anemias against David's victory over Goliath and the hit song that became #1 on the Billboard charts, "Saul has killed his thousands but David his tens of thousands," Saul just could not take it. David was a man in his cabinet who was outshining him. Saul started wondering if David was in his cabinet but not in his corner.

Moses, that great emancipator of the Jews, gave us the Ten Commandments; in it, he tells us not to covet the things of others. Since Putin has had his eye on Ukraine, it has caused much devastation and death to men, women, boys, and girls by bombing schools, hospitals, apartment complexes, and vital infrastructure. War is always about power and domination. War involves taking someone else's resources, finances, influence, and power. Whatever happens stems from envy or the belief that you deserve what others have.

The first murder crime scene in the Bible was because of envy. Cain killed his brother Abel because he was envious of God's acceptance of his brother's offering over his. Envy led to the tragic deaths of Samson and his contemporaries.

Consider two little teardrops floating down the river of life; one teardrop asked the other, "Who are you?"

"I am a teardrop from a girl who loved and lost a man. And who are?"

The first teardrop replied, "I am a teardrop from the girl who got him."

Life is like that; we cry over things we cannot have, but we might cry twice if we receive them and later lose them.

In Putin's case, the virtue that should have been exhibited instead of envy should have been contentment. If Putin had displayed contentment, he would have never invaded the sovereign nation of Ukraine. Putin has tried to rewrite Russia's history of glory long buried in the ashes of the dateless past. Putin has changed his reason for his invasion so often that it's hard to keep up with all his fairy tales. They are all lies. Contentment causes us to admit that God is the one who ultimately dispenses the blessing and that He is no respecter of person. God will always do what is right. He rains on the just and the unjust and will give all his people the blessings he desires. May we all be satisfied with the benefits and the blessings.

Lust: In the autopsy of Samson and his women, passion shows up on the death certificate, and another disease contributed to their demise. Lust is an excessive craving to satisfy sexual desire and a hunger for material or worldly things.

Lust and Its roots can be found in the production of the heart. It is what one wants and is a must-have attitude. It is selfish and tetters on greed. Samson and the women in his life were in the same boat. Unfortunately, it sunk their boats.

The world does not want to hear it, let alone accept it, but sex was designed within the confines of marriage. Generally, sex falls into two categories: procreation and recreation. We will be held accountable to the one who created us. We should always keep sex within the parameters of marriage and understand its purpose. The same God who plugged the stars in their glittering sockets and made them look like jewels resting on the dark velvet of the night, painted the blue dome without a step ladder or a brush, deserves our respect. If we respect God's design for a man and a woman, we will be in balance with His divine will. What a Mighty God we serve. We owe God everything because he is our creator, and we are his artistry created in Christ Jesus. **(Eph 2:10)**

I Thessalonians 4:7-8 "For God hath not called us unto uncleanness but unto holiness. Therefore, he despises not man, but God, who hath also given unto us his Holy Spirit." Lust only seeks to please oneself, whereas love is always mutual. We usually think of lust as beginning purely sexual. It can also be an intense craving for fame, money, alcohol, and drugs. Samson and his women all wanted sex as the main entrée, and anything else strongly desired was the dessert. They should have shown self-control and discretion, which would have led to a better example for themselves and the communities in which they lived. It has been said that Lust is the craving for the salt of a man dying of thirst.

Anger: The next cause of death I would like to suggest is anger, primarily directed toward Samson. Samson showed a total disregard for keeping his emotions in check. He was hot-tempered, and in many of his many escapades, things did not go as he expected. He would set fields on fire and kill you if you outsmarted him with his riddles. His actions were just ridiculous for a grown man. He certainly would be something to live with as a spouse. I am sure if Sistergirl burns up the supper, it will probably be a long night for sure.

Anger is one of the seven deadly sins. Anger is not all bad when directed in the proper direction. In **Ephesians 4:26,** the ESV says, "Be angry and do not sin; do not let the sun go down on your anger."

Phyllis Diller, an old-time comedian I remember many years ago, had a saying for couples: "Never go to bed mad. Stay up and fight." Anger is always an uncontrolled thing that is wrath and, if not subdued, can lead to violence. With all of the gun violence in America, it is evident that we have an anger problem. People are angry about many things: their jobs, politicians and their policies, abortion rights, wars, the left's politics, and the right's politics. They are downright angry.

As I have said before, being angry is not all bad. Jesus showed divine anger when he saw religious leaders using the house of God as a place of merchandise and grift. **(Matthew 21:12-13)** Jesus was correct in his actions. Jesus did not condone using His father's house as a place to make money at the expense of the people trying to obey the fundamentals of the law.

I can identify with Samson; after all, he was an only child, as am I. I am also adopted, and to this day, I still do not know my biological parents. I have had the pleasure of being the center of attention for most of my life. In my childhood days, I would usually get my way. Samson was the kind of fellow if you play ball with him and win, he will take his ball and go home angrily.

Samson's life shows us how gracious God is and how foolish we can be. God should have fired Samson, but he did not and kept him on the job. He ruled as a judge for some twenty years. God knew how the story would end. God is just so merciful. The lesson for men is that our unbridled anger can quickly destroy a relationship. It can destroy a career and the very thing we love so dearly. Anger causes us to make impulse decisions and wander in the fog rather than walking in the light. God is light. **(1John 1:5)**

True story: I came home one day and found a pair of size fourteen shoes in my kitchen, and I asked my children Symone and Simeon whose shoes they were. They both said they did not know. Well, I knew they were not mine! I wear size nine and a half. Ok, I am getting hotter by the minute, and I think some man has been to my house without my knowledge. Up pulls my wife from work, and I hear her car pulling into the garage. Sitting in the kitchen, I asked her whose shoes are these. She keeps walking and says, "I don't know."

But before I went coo coo, sho-nuff. I heard the Lord say, "Robert, calm down. The shoes in the house are your barber's shoes he dropped off because the shoe shop next to your office was closed, and he asked you if he could give them to you to give to Larry at the shop, remember?" I broke down and cried. I was acting so silly in my anger that I was about to blow up the house and everybody in it because I forgot how the shoes got there. The devil will use anything he can to destroy us if we let him. Samson should have gotten some anger management training. He should have allowed one of the Fruit of the Spirit (self-control) **Galatians 5:19-21** guide and control his life. If he had done so, certain things would have and could have turned out far differently.

When the Spirit of the Living God controls us, we will have control over sinful desires. Self-control gives us the power to say no to the devil and yes to God's will.

Greed: Finally, greed was the straw that broke the camel's back in the unfolding drama of the judgeship of Samson. Greed is an excessive desire to have more and more and can never be satisfied. Greed is usually associated with money. But greed covers more than just money. Greed covers much ground. The desire for fame, power, recognition, and titles is just a few. Samson's greed harbored the strong desire to have the same nationality of prohibited women in his life, the Philistine women. All of them were women who worked in the red-light district. Samson loved to do what God commanded him not to do.

Amazingly, almost all the women that Samson encountered were exclusively motivated by financial gain and power. The Philistine women's connection with him gave them access to status and a chance to meddle in Israel's destiny through manipulation. This motivation was not for the betterment of Israel but coerced essentially by the Philistine lords who used them to gain an advantage.

Chapter Seven

Finding Love in the Electronic Age

The World's Way to Marriage: The Electronic Age

Online Dating Statistics-2022-2023 Trends Report

- The global market size of online dating is $12.89 billion.

- There are more than 8,000 online dating sites globally.

- 7.86 million users use Tinder in the US

- Approximately 323 million people worldwide use dating apps.

- 84% of online daters are looking for a romantic relationship.

- 24% are looking for a sexual relationship.

- Around 42% of users are looking for marriage.

- Almost 14% of online daters marry someone they met online.

The internet is a technological marvel. It was created in the 1960s at the height of the Cold War and the race between two superpowers, the United States and the USSR. The US needed a way to communicate in case of a nuclear attack.

The United States government initially used the Internet for its own purposes, but it later branched out to other uses. When the government no longer needs something, it usually passes it on to the private sector. This is how the internet became a multi-faceted tool for many different purposes today.

The internet has been a blessing and a curse. It has brought progress to many areas of our lives but has also been used for evil purposes. Where there is progress, there is often also degeneration. The internet is a double-edged sword that can be used for good or bad.

God never intended for us to find a mate by impersonal means through bots and artificial intelligence. Social media has allowed us to become instant celebrities overnight. There is nothing that takes the place of interpersonal relationships. We text instead of picking up the phone. We have done so much that our society has lost the skill of human connections. TikTok, Instagram, Twitter, and Facebook allow us to become cowards as we hide behind the facade of a computer screen. We photoshopped our pictures; making ourselves more appealing is the day's vogue.

The electronic age robs a couple, a business, and a workforce of the most essential skills in the universe. It is basic communication—the ability to communicate and develop interpersonal relationships. Texting may be convenient, but it is so impersonal and aloof and, over time, destroys our ability to understand the message as well as the messenger. Texting reduces a person to characters, letters, and emojis. All human beings and relationships require more than hand movement on a keypad or iPhone tapping. It requires human interaction. When we use facial expressions, hand gestures, voice tone, and all the other visuals, it helps us better understand what is being communicated.

My daughter Symone, when she must take care of some business, she is so reluctant. She says to me, "Dad, what do I say." Texting makes us struggle to communicate clearly and speak our minds freely. The electronic age has sped up some things but slowed down others. Our phones have made us lazy. We don't have to answer. We can text, ignore, or call back at a time convenient for us. I guess it's not all bad, but it causes us to reduce people to things and objects begging for our attention.

Online dating is a new thing that rarely leads to long-lasting relationships. Many of the Facebook profiles are false and, at best, fairytale. If the relationship starts with lies, it will end with lies. One of the downsides of online dating is that you do not know what you are getting on the other side of the screen. Deception is sure to manifest, and when it does, it snowballs into a web of distrust. Even in traditional dating, we hide our true selves.

The web is filled with impersonators and a sea of criminal activity, and if you ever get caught in their net, it is challenging to get out. The theft of your personal information is always at risk. Are you aware that you can purchase just about anything on the web with a click of a button? Usernames, passwords, and drugs can all be bought at your fingertips. You can meet a guy or a gal as well.

Phishing also is a trick to get your personal information. In the area of online dating, every precaution must be taken. I strongly do not recommend this type of single and searching novel. I believe the old-fashioned way of meet and greet still works today and should be the preferred method.

I learned the hard way about deception in graduate school at JSU. It was not through the internet, but a hard lesson on how to be fooled online and offline! Buyer beware. So, what happened? So glad you asked! If I had a hard lesson in cold, brutal deception, this was it. It was not online, but it was on my mind.

I had worked mowing yards and washing cars all summer to start working on my master's degree. My rich aunts had even given me money to further my education. It was December 1980. I had arrived in Jackson, MS, and I was staying with Dr. Joseph Sutton, a retired educator, a wealthy man, and a beloved friend of my dad. I loved chilling at Kmart and walking around a large department store. So, I was walking around in the store and was met by a man who had a Jamaican accent.

I later learned that his name was Pierre. He pulled out a wad of money that was one-hundred-dollar bills. He got my attention! He said that he had just gotten to the States and did not know how to open a bank account, and if I helped him, he would give me $1000! Now that gets my attention! So, he follows me to my car and says, "Put your money in this bag with mine to prove I can trust you." He was sitting in the car's back seat, so I could not see what he was really doing. He handed me a bag and said to lock it in the glove compartment. I did. He then began to cry and said his wife had cancer and was dying. He stepped away from the car to return to Kmart and said he would return shortly, but I guess you know he did not. I waited for over an hour and finally got up enough nerve to open the glove box and see what was in the bag. It was nothing but shredded paper. I had been hit by what the old folks called in my day, a pigeon dropper. I lost all my money, and he did not take it. I gave it to him. Deception is a spirit that causes you to feed on greed, pleasure, and the thrill of getting something for nothing. All I was thinking about was the extra $1000 that I thought I was about to get, and I ended up losing everything. Be careful online or as well as your in-person interactions, especially with strangers.

Without question, online dating consumers are driven by the desire for sex that feeds on looks, and if looks alone are the foundation for your relationships, then they are doomed from the start.

We all change as we age. The wrinkles, weight gain, health challenges, hair issues replaced with wigs, you name it. The changes will come with an endless catalog. Again, I say, buyer beware. If it's too good to be true, take it from me. It most certainly is.

Consider some more interesting facts on online dating.

Online dating and finding a partner through these platforms are more common among adults who are younger or lesbian, gay or bisexual

% of U.S. adults who say they ...

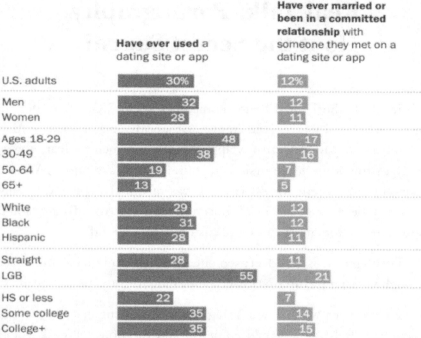

	Have ever used a dating site or app	Have ever married or been in a committed relationship with someone they met on a dating site or app
U.S. adults	30%	12%
Men	32	12
Women	28	11
Ages 18-29	48	17
30-49	38	16
50-64	19	7
65+	13	5
White	29	12
Black	31	12
Hispanic	28	11
Straight	28	11
LGB	55	21
HS or less	22	7
Some college	35	14
College+	35	15

Note: Whites and blacks include only non-Hispanics. Hispanics are of any race. LGB indicates those who identify as lesbian, gay or bisexual. Those who did not give an answer are not shown.
Source: Survey of U.S. adults conducted Oct. 16-28, 2019.
"The Virtues and Downsides of Online Dating"

PEW RESEARCH CENTER

I believe the traditional way to find a mate is God's design, and the sooner we get back to the old fashion basics of courtship, the better our society will become.

Chapter Eight

Real Talk: Pornography Is it the Secret Sauce?

In 2021, the United States companies spent 285 billion dollars on advertising. Pictures and images of goods and services entice consumers to pay. Advertisers appeal to things such as fear, anger, greed, or the desire to be first, to mention a few. As a retired Allstate insurance sales agent for 30 years, I was taught that people usually don't buy because of no need, hurry, money, or trust. To act, some motivating factors must cause the customer to respond.

Pornography is an advertisement that seeks to induce you to act through viewing pictures or images appealing to some unmet need.

I remember when I was a high school student, Jell-O was big. Every time Bill Cosby would come on and promote Jell-O, I would immediately run to the store to buy some. That is the power of advertising at work. Pornography pushes our buttons and hurts the psyche, family, and marriage. It is sinful, and it appeals to man's worst desires.

Harvard Professor Kevin Majeres has performed studies that support the effect pornography causes. Writing on the blog: "**Purity is Possible,**" he explains the effect of porn with repeated exposure. He used rats to test various outcomes. The findings were terrific as well as alarming.

Consider the findings from the study:

"Scientists have discovered that if you place a male rat in a cage with a receptive female, they will mate; but once done, the male rat will not mate more times, even if the female is still receptive. He loses all sexual interest. But if, right after he finishes with the first female, you put in a second receptive female, he will immediately mate again, and again, a third, and so on, until he nearly dies. This effect has been found in every animal studied. This is called the Coolidge effect."

The lower part of our brain is so sensitive that it cannot tell the difference between reality and non-reality. It sees both as accurate. That said, the images of porn place us in a make-believe and fantasy world. If we are exposed to pornographic images of the opposite sex repeatedly, eventually, your mate will no longer arouse you sexually; only those pictures that you feed your mind will stimulate you. Over time you will become so desensitized that you will have little desire for your mate or spouse. This is how pornography alters your behavior without you realizing what is happening.

Pornography is one of Satan's many ways to steer you away from having genuine, wholesome relationships. Facebook is filled with images of women shaking their rumps, exposing themselves, and saying suggestive overtones, "Come, get me," these are what I call "soft" porn that nevertheless leads to destructive outcomes. Women are using the platforms of Facebook and TikTok to get as many clicks as possible to get the *Benjamins* rolling in. Be mindful of the games people play. They don't want you; they want your money and as many clicks and views as they can accumulate. This is how to get paid.

Furthermore, look what Harvard professor Kevin Majeres found concerning dopamine:

"Dopamine is the drug of desire – when you see something desirable, your brain pours out dopamine, saying "Go for it! Do whatever it takes!" Dopamine fixes your attention on that desirable object, giving you your power of concentration...

So, when someone clicks and sees a new pornographic image, his lower brain thinks this is the real thing, this is the lady he must win over with all his might, and so he gets an enormous dopamine flood in his upper brain, causing a wild amount of electrical energy.

This first exposure to a new female who is a potential mate wasn't something that happened a lot to our ancestors, maybe only once in their lives, so the brain thinks this is a big deal. It doesn't know that now the game has completely changed: it doesn't understand that these are virtual females only; so with each new one, it causes another flood of dopamine, time after time, click after click, as long as he continues. It's a dopamine binge."

This study is quite interesting, but I will repeat alarming. Information is power. We should do better when we learn better. Porn puts you on a merry-go-round, in my own words. These harmful pictures destroy receptors, and you need more of what you don't have because, over time, dopamine will be depleted from your brain. And all the Viagra in the world won't change that. The subtle part is that it is causing great harm without your knowledge.

Viagra works when you are stimulated. The bottom line is that pornography is not the secret sauce. It never was and never will be. Pornography will eventually cause your love life to run in reverse. Instead of building a love that will last, it will be only fringes of lust that will soon fizzle out.

Pornography is one of the most dangerous ways for a person to spend their time. Famous restaurants boast of their unique delights and seasonings. Every food establishment believes they have a secret sauce that answers all tastes. Pornography makes a poor attempt to satisfy the preferences of the flesh. It makes the imagination run wild and damages real-life experiences. It puts a person in a make-believe world, where the screen of their mind becomes the theater, and you become the director of the cinematography of what your heart can imagine.

What is so dangerous about this? It creates expectations in a relationship that are impossible to meet.

Television makes us think this is how it is, but it's all a fairy tale. It's a script. The tale is on you if you are stupid enough to believe the script. It's not real. You need to flip the script when you see that you are getting hooked.

I always hated watching TV with my daddy; he never cared much about television and never learned to tell the difference between a commercial and an actual television program.

When pornography is a pastime recreation, it affects one's view of reality. You can't tell where the unreal stops and the real begins.

The sole purpose of pornography is to stimulate the senses through pictures. Because of electronic media, pornography is easily accessible.

The Bible condemns pornography. **Ephesians 5:3-4** says, "Let sexual immorality and every sort of uncleanness or greediness not even be mentioned among you, a just as is proper for holy people; neither shameful conduct nor foolish talking nor obscene jesting—things that are not befitting—but rather the giving of thanks."

Watching porn may be fun and tension-relieving, but it is not goal-achieving.

Some couples watch pornography as a type of aphrodisiac to jump-start a romantic evening. While at first, it may appear to work harmlessly on the surface, it's the picture on the screen that is exciting you and not the one lying beside you. It is a false flag and a red flag. I hate to tell you the truth, but you are fooling yourself.

Wholesome relationships must be cultivated and not motivated by external prompts. It is counterfeit love. If couples are not excited about being with each other through touch, smell, and sight nothing else really matters.

I believe that six Greek love languages must be cultivated to sustain a balanced lifelong romantic relationship. They are **Agape** (God's Love) and **Eros** (Romantic love such as hugging, kissing etc.) **Epithumia** (Sexual), **Storge'**(Fellowship is the enjoyment of just hanging around the person and spending time with them,) **Phileo** (Friendship and having a listening ear), and lastly (**Ludus**) Playful love, flirtatious gestures and touching, and sexual shout outs that have emotional connections and strong vibes.

Relationships driven solely by the physical will soon burn out like a candle and wear out like a cheap suit. The lasting ones are sustained by genuineness and Godly principles. We can never know and experience true love until we know the God of Love.

1 John 4:8 Says, "He that loveth not knoweth not God; for God is love."

Chapter Nine

Marriage: The Dinosaur of the Last Frontier

Marriage has been described as the relationship of "two reasonable human beings who have agreed to abide by each other's intolerable."

Today's definition of marriage has changed tremendously over the past decade. Globally, it no longer has a consensus in meaning. With these factors encroaching upon the landscape of marriage in our world, we can understand why the biblical concept of marriage is swiftly becoming a dinosaur right before our very eyes.

Marriage as we know it is swiftly changing. Ironically, archeologists discovered that dinosaurs died out due to their inability to change and adapt. It appears as if marriage is a dinosaur that is having difficulty adjusting to new norms and the twists and turns of marriage.

Let's be honest, when was the last time you attended a wedding? If you have a local newspaper, when did you last see a wedding announcement in your local paper? When was the last time you got an invitation to a wedding or bought a gift for newlyweds? It is rare. I am a pastor, and it seems to be on the pages of antiquity. Marriage is not an event that appears to be the going thing today. Shacking or casual living arrangements seem to be the tide of least resistance today. It is the buy product of the lack of commitment. Many living arrangements today are centered around a type of open-door policy. Come and go as you like.

In America, we strive for independence and doing our own thing with the freedom to come and go as we please and do as we please or a laissez-faire attitude. Some see marriage as a drag on their independence. After all, why get married anyway, some ask? Why buy the cow when you can get her milk-free, right? Ouch! I am sure you have heard that before, but there is a great deal of truth to that bold statement.

Furthermore, there could be another reason we see so few notices in the local paper. Many are taking the option of going to the justice of the peace, and the couple preferred not to publish it in the local paper. This is a mistake when a couple does not print the marriage in the local paper. The publicized marriage establishes you in the eyes of your community as a couple. This causes the community to recognize and accept you as husband and wife. It also helps to ward off the paramours that still think you are on the market and in hot pursuit.

I overheard a judge informing a couple of the fees he charged for performing the wedding. He said, "I got two prices, one for $5 and one for $10." The couple asked what was the difference. "The Judge said at the $5.00 wedding, I just do the ceremony and only what the law requires, but at the $10.00 wedding, I sing." They said, "Oh, if that is the case, we will take the $5.00 wedding." This probably will be a shocking statement, but here it goes. A public wedding ceremony is not for the couple. It is for the community. The community must witness and verify that you are married and no longer single. It is how the community is put on notice to respect the couple becoming one and ultimately growing to become a family.

For the record, a wedding ceremony can range from simple to extravagant. It has become quite common today to see couples take the Lord's Supper or Holy Communion. However, you wish to refer to it. I studied this inclusion in weddings and am convinced it is inappropriate. While, as a matter of optics, it may look beautiful, it does not belong in a wedding ceremony. I strongly condemn this practice.

Furthermore, inappropriate music during the ceremony should not dignify this unique service. It is a sacred service and should never take on the atmosphere of a secular service.

The Lord's Supper is a memorial representing the end of Jesus's life and a word picture of his death. This is antithetical because a wedding marks the beginning of a life and not the end of a life. If a couple seeks to symbolize oneness at a wedding, may I suggest:

Two beautiful goblets symbolize the (Bride and Groom) and one bottle of red wine symbolizes (Love)

One large glass of beautiful crystal glass (symbolizing unity)

The couple pour each other a glass of wine into goblets

The bride and groom take a sip and toast together, and then …

Empty their goblets into the crystal glass, symbolizing becoming one.

In the past, marriage was for security. Today's professional woman has money, a home, an automobile, and interests. If she wants children, she has many options. She can either adopt one or pay for In-vitro-fertilization. Also, she can get pregnant, isolate the man, and limit his involvement in her life and the child's.

With so many options, we can see why marriage is not as attractive as it once was years ago. It appears that marriage is indeed the dinosaur of the last frontier. That road is narrow, and there are few there you find on that road.

History records that the biggest boom in marriage occurred after WWII. It has seen a steady decline since then. Sociologists have studied the reason why. These are some of the plausible explanations. As previously stated, increased independence and the constant push for gender equality.

Moreover, between 1990 and 2019, marriages decreased from 9.8 per 1000 people to 6.1. Nick Wolfinger, a Family and Consumer Studies professor at the University of Utah, suggests people are delaying marriage. This shows up in the data as declining growth.

In addition, Brian Willoughby, a professor at Brigham Young University's School of Family Life, says, "The delay is due to changing values, the acceptable lifestyle of couples living together and the belief that marriage is not necessary to have a healthy fulfilling partnered life."

I believe relationships that last swing on the hinges of commitment. It swings one way, and then it turns another. No marriage will be perfect; there must be a give and take, and it's not my way or the highway.

Many couples today want the option to get out of the relationship without any hassle or legal repercussions if things don't go as expected. So, they just "shack," as we say in my neck of the woods.

Society has become more accepting of this lifestyle of shacking than it used to be, and as a result, it is being widely practiced, sadly, in Christian churches as well. I often encounter the single and searching woman who desires marriage but does not want children. This trend has had an impact on public educational school systems. Schools are paid by their state departments based on the average daily attendance (ADA).

When there is a decline in the student population in school, schools close, and teachers are laid off. This happens across Mississippi, especially in the Mississippi Delta region. Abortion also affects population growth among all demographics. Non-whites run a higher percentage per thousand than any other demographics. Abortion and healthcare issues continue to be the elephant in the room.

Marriage is still the fundamental pillar of American society, and it will be necessary to reverse the trends of marriage decline if we are to have a sustainable society, a strong America, and a beacon of hope we all have come to rely on.

In addition, the educational status of an individual has an impact on marriage as well. The more educated a person is, the more likely they will get married and stay married. Let's face it, wedding and the total package that come with it, such as children, their support, their education needs k-12 and college and postgraduate if desired, wanting a home and its demands and your own time for some relaxation is a lot to be considered financially. Marriage still has a chance to survive, but only if we give it a chance.

As a person ages, there seems to be tremendous pressure and a mad rush to get married. When this mindset takes place, it will mostly lead to an unsuccessful marriage and, ultimately, divorce. In the United States, a marriage lasts about 20 years. That said, the divorce rate in the United States is over 50 percent. There is a huge casualty rate of getting hitched today. Marriage is not for everybody. Look at what Paul writes in **1 Corinthians 7:1-17**

"Now, getting down to the questions you asked in your letter. First, Is it a good thing to have sexual relations?

Certainly—but only within a specific context. It's good for a man to have a wife and a woman to have a husband. Sexual drives are strong, but marriage is strong enough to contain them and provide a balanced and fulfilling sexual life in a world of sexual disorder. The marriage bed must be a place of mutuality—the husband seeking to satisfy his wife, the wife seeking to meet her husband. Marriage is not a place to "stand up for your rights." Marriage is a decision to serve the other, whether in bed or out. Abstaining from sex is permissible if you both agree to it and if it's for prayer and fasting—but only for such times. Then come back together again. Satan has an ingenious way of tempting us when we least expect it. I'm not, understand, commanding these periods of abstinence, providing my best counsel if you should choose them.

Sometimes, I wish everyone were single like me—a simpler life in many ways! But celibacy is not for everyone any more than marriage is. God gives the gift of a single life to some and the gift of married life to others.

I do, though, tell the unmarried and widows that singleness might well be the best thing for them, as it has been for me. But if they can't manage their desires and emotions, they should go ahead and get married. The difficulties of marriage are preferable by far to a sexually tortured life as a single.

And if you are married, stay married. This is the Master's command, not mine. If a wife should leave her husband, she must either remain single or return and make things right with him. And a husband has no right to get rid of his wife.

For the rest of you in mixed marriages—Christian married to non-Christian—we have no explicit command from the Master. So, this is what you must do. If you are a man with a wife who is not a believer but still wants to live with you, hold on to her. If you are a woman with a husband who is not a believer, but he wants to live with you, hold on to him. The unbelieving husband shares, to an extent, in the holiness of his wife, and the righteousness of her husband likewise touches the skeptical wife. Otherwise, your children would be left out; as it is, they also are included in the spiritual purposes of God.

On the other hand, if the unbelieving spouse walks out, you've got to let them go. You don't have to hold on desperately. God has called us to make the best of it as peacefully as possible. You never know, wife: How you handle this might bring your husband back to you and God. You never know, husband: How you take this might bring your wife back to you and God.

And don't wish you were somewhere else or with someone else. Where you are right now is God's place for you. Live and obey and love and believe right there. God, not your marital status, defines your life. Don't think I'm being harder on you than on the others. I give this same counsel in all the churches."

We all should be encouraged because it may look bleak, but it is not all a lost cause. The Bible says that he who finds a wife finds a good thing. The hard part is in finding that good thing. In real estate, it is all about location, location, location. We can look for Mr. or Ms. Right in all the wrong places. God will meet your needs and lead you to that special someone who will be the answer to your fulfillment and joy. God is fully aware of all your wants, conditions, and desires. He can make significant and glorious things happen for us and bless us if we place our trust in the Lord.

Chapter Ten

The Fruit Basket Every Home Needs

If you think men and women want different things from each other to be happy, you are probably in good company. On the contrary, after 35 years of marriage and over 25 years of pastoring, I am convinced that men and women all want the desired outcome. Adam and Eve ate fruit that was not on the menu, which caused great stress in their diet and affected the whole world. Sin and death were the result of their consumption. However, there is desirable fruit that every couple should have in the house and on their menu. The needs of humanity are universal in all parts of the world.

This story concerns a very busy business person with a wife. He just could not, for some reason, determine what was wrong with her. He did everything he could to find out why his wife was never happy, regardless of what he said and did. So, he concluded that she needed to see a doctor. In private, he told the doctor all of her symptoms and all the things he had tried to do and that all his efforts failed. So, he asked the doctor to see if he could find out what was wrong with his wife. So, the doctor's receptionist took down the details concerning her symptoms, her insurance information was also retrieved, and she waited her turn to be called. After about 40 minutes, she was called in to see the doctor.

Well, she went in to see the doctor, and the doctor examined her and asked several questions; some were quite intense, personal, and intimate. So, the doctor started running his hands through her hair, caressing her back, kissing her gently, and saying nice things in a soft tone. After about 25 minutes, the doctor came out, and her husband noticed a tremendous improvement in her countenance. She was glowing and smiling. He said, "Show me what you did." Well, the doctor said I don't want to do that. I don't think that would be a good idea. You must, replied her husband. I am paying for this office visit and demand that you tell me what you did to her. So reluctantly, the doctor stepped back and showed the husband all he did. And then the doctor said, "Now you are going to need to do what I did at least three times a week." The husband said, "Doc, if that's what it takes, I can gladly bring her in only on Tuesdays and Thursdays!".

Sometimes, we fail to realize the most simplistic things our spouse needs, and after we discover them, we fail to fulfill those needs. Let us not be guilty of doing our part to make the marriage successful. When the nine fruits of the spirit manifest, they release the nature of Jesus, and his nature completely satisfies all that a man or a woman needs.

Therefore, the fruit of the Spirit is comprehensive in terms of what couples should desire. These nine fruits say it all. Let's look at them and apply them. They are in clusters of threes, building on each other. Each gift gives us the power to be victorious in our relationships at home and abroad.

Jesus said I am the vine; you are the branches. When we abide in him, we bear fruit. It's a natural process. Since Jesus says we are the branches, this is where the fruit grows. The fruit we produce is not for us to consume ourselves but for others to enjoy. We are picked out to be picked on.

The fruit of the Spirit is the manifestation of the Nature of Christ. You have heard I am sure of the "Gifts of the Spirit" 1 Corinthians 12:7-11

"But the manifestation of the Spirit is given to every man to profit withal.

[8] For to one is given by the Spirit the word of wisdom, to another the word of knowledge by the same Spirit.

[9] To another faith by the same Spirit; to another the gifts of healing by the same Spirit.

[10] To another the working of miracles; to another prophecy; to another discerning of spirits; to another diverse kind of tongues; to another the interpretation of tongues:

[11] But all these worketh that one and the selfsame Spirit, dividing to every man severally as he will."

The gifts are to be **received**; nothing is to be done to get them, whereas the Fruit of the Spirit must be **developed** and **cultivated**. Marriage is a work in progress, a never fully developed photograph.

In photography, a picture undergoes development in the darkroom before being brought into the light. Similarly, our growth and development must go through difficult phases in the "darkroom" of life before we fully mature into the beautiful picture we are meant to become.

Fruit must grow, its roots must take shape, it must receive rain, and some occasional pruning may be necessary. Whatever the case may be, it is a process. It does not grow overnight. It takes time. Marriage takes time, ladies and gentlemen, to develop.

My parents had a pecan tree in our yard, and children in the neighborhood would sneak in it when they thought nobody was home. And as the old folk would say, they loved to "chunk" in the tree. The world will certainly "chunk" at you if your life(**tree**) has fruit. Rejoice because you are growing to maturity in the Lord and have value and productiveness.

Let us turn to the fruit and look at them and see how blessed and enriched our lives will become after their manifestation. There are (9) Fruit of the Spirit. The first one is foundational. Let us examine them and their significance in the lives of a believer. Notice I said fruit, singular.

The Fruit of the Spirit is considered one. Although 9 manifest themselves, they are one in clusters of threes!

The Nature of Jesus

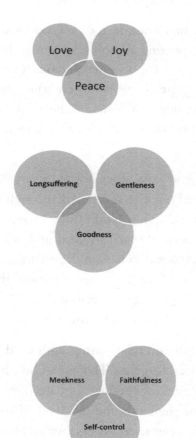

The Fruit of the Spirit (The Nature of Jesus)

Galatians 5:22-25 "22 But the fruit of the Spirit is love, joy, peace, longsuffering, gentleness, goodness, faith,

23 Meekness, temperance: against such there is no law.

24 And they that are Christ's have crucified the flesh with the affections and lusts.

25 If we live in the Spirit, let us also walk in the Spirit."

Let's look at them step by step prayerfully:

1. Love is the first fruit, agape or God's love. This type of love pours out, never expecting anything in return. It is unselfish love. It seeks the highest good for another person. The Greek word that is translated here is **agape.** It means to entertain, welcome, be fond of, and love dearly. The death of Jesus on the cross was to show God the Father's highest expression of His love for a sinful world in need of a loving savior.

Romans 5:5 "And hope does not put us to shame, because God's love has been poured out into our hearts through the Holy Spirit, who has been given to us." This Godly love extends upward as well as outward. It is our vertical reach to God and our horizontal reach to each other. This relationship is foundational and must be a constant longing to seek God's love, love our mate and those around us, and develop healthy and productive relationships. Love is the first fruit. God is Love; we must have him before any other fruit grows.

Our communion and relationship with God hinge on the degree to which we have been forgiven. That could be why some people make more noise than others in worship; they have more to be grateful for due to the height of their sins and the level of forgiveness they need. The more we confess our need for his love and forgiveness in our lives, the louder our praise should be.

The Apostle Paul taught: "**1 Corinthians 13,** If I speak in the tongues[a] of men or angels, but do not have love, I am only a resounding gong or a clanging cymbal. 2 If I have the gift of prophecy and can fathom all mysteries and all knowledge, and if I have a faith that can move mountains, but do not have love, I am nothing. ³ If I give all I possess to the poor and give over my body to hardship that I may boast,[b] but do not have love, I gain nothing.

⁴ Love is patient; love is kind. It does not envy, it does not boast, it is not proud. ⁵ It does not dishonor others, is not self-seeking, is not easily angered, and keeps no record of wrongs. ⁶ Love does not delight in evil but rejoices with the truth. ⁷ It always protects, always trusts, always hopes, always perseveres.⁸ Love never fails. But where there are prophecies, they will cease; where there are tongues, they will be stilled; where there is knowledge, it will pass away. ⁹ For we know in part, and we prophesy in part, ¹⁰ but when completeness comes, what is in part disappears. ¹¹ When I was a child, I talked like a child, I thought like a child, I reasoned like a child. When I became a man, I put the ways of childhood behind me. ¹² For now, we see only a reflection as in a mirror; then we shall see face to face. Now I know in part; then I shall know fully, even as I am fully known.

¹³ And now these three remain faith, hope, and love. But the greatest of these is love."

When our relationships are right with God, they will be in harmony with all other relationships.

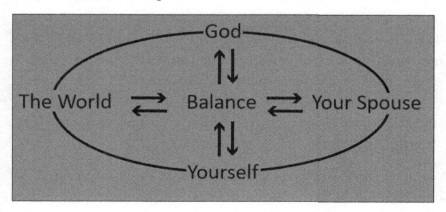

The flow of vertical and horizontal relationships.

2. Joy is that internal virtue that is not affected by the external noise of the world. It cannot be disturbed by what takes place in the world. Joy differs from happiness; its blessed state is not determined by the shifting sand of time or changing world winds. Because our anchor is in Jesus, our joy never changes. Knowing that all good and perfect gifts come from God and that nothing can separate us, his love causes all grace to abound toward us. We are in His hand, and our hand is in His.

Joy is the inner strength that empowers us to remain steadfast, unmovable, and always abounding in the Lord. The trial of our faith pushes us to go on to maturity.

Mountains are rough in their terrain. If they were smooth, they would be almost impossible to climb. Their roughness gives our feet a place to get a grip and our hands to handle things. Joy is the big dipper that draws from the well of salvation in Christ Jesus.

I Peter 1:8 "Though you have not seen him, you love him; and even though you do not see him now, you believe in him and are filled with an inexpressible and glorious joy,"

3. Peace This is the tranquility of the mind, body, and soul. It is the absolute confidence that God is in control. We are in his will, and he has promised to take care of all our needs from now until eternity. There is the peace of God and the peace with God. Peace of God means that because of my relationship with him, my very being is settled, and I am no longer at war with Him and His kingdom agenda. The peace with God is knowing I am a child of God, not a candidate for hell but a citizen of heaven and listed in the Lamb's Book of Life.

Peace is that onboard umpire that calls the balls and strikes in our lives. Peace assures us that the decisions we make on behalf of ourselves and our family align with God's will. When we can't rest and have no peace, it is a sign that we are out of bounds with God's plan. Furthermore, you can never have peace with others without peace within yourself. It's not "What is your problem?" No, the problem is with you! We do not have to stress out about the things we cannot control. Our victory is in Jesus. Be of good cheer, Jesus says, "I have overcome the world." **John 16:33**. Jesus was hung up for all our hangups. Walk in freedom and live in freedom.

John 14:27 "Peace I leave with you, the peace I give to you; not as the world gives do I give to you. Let not your heart be troubled, neither let it be afraid."

1 Thessalonians 5:23 "May God himself, the God of peace, sanctify you through and through. May your whole spirit, soul, and body be kept blameless at the coming of our Lord Jesus Christ."

4. Long-suffering is the ability to put up with some stuff. It is the skill of having patience, stick-to-it-ness, and being slow to take offense and slow to anger. It is the supernatural ability to stand tough situations where you would lose your cool under normal circumstances.

Longsuffering allows you to stand under pressure, hardness, persecution, distress, and trouble yet maintain steadfastness and patience. This fruit always helps you walk through the valley of adversity and not get knocked down in battle. Longsuffering allows you to come out on top as a victor and not a victim.

The primary function of Longsuffering is endurance. Endurance is the absence of having a pity party, suffering from depression, and becoming resentful of the situation. Paul is an excellent example of one who was a long-distance runner. He is the exemplar of endurance.

Christ taught us to be steadfast in endurance: "And all will hate you for My name's sake. But he who endures to the end will be saved."

Matthew 10:22

Another function of endurance is to claim the blessed promises of God without having shipwreck faith, including but not limited to obtaining wealth.

Deut 8:18 "And you shall remember the Lord your God, for *it is* He who gives you the power to get wealth, that He may establish His covenant which He swore to your fathers, as *it is* this day."

Hebrews 6:12-15 says, 12 "We do not want you to become lazy, but to imitate those who through faith and patience inherit what has been promised. 13 When God made his promise to Abraham, since there was no one greater for him to swear by, he swore by himself, 14 saying, I will surely bless you and give you many descendants. 15 And so after waiting patiently, Abraham received what was promised."

Lastly, endurance allows you to forgive when hurt and move past your old wounds. Forgiveness is letting go and letting God. He is the only one that can genuinely heal us. We sometimes receive many injuries on the battlefield of life; if we were on an X-ray machine, many of our wounds would not show up. There are some places that the most precise surgeon cannot possibly reach. In this case, only God can reach the unreachable places where we are hurt. Jesus is the Great Physician who can do what no other power can.

Ephesians 4:23 "Be kind and compassionate to one another, forgiving each other, just as in Christ God forgave you."

5. Gentleness is knowing how to act in all situations. They say it's being a gentleman or a gentle lady on the U.S. House of Representatives floor. Furthermore, it has the moral aptitude, a compass that motivates you to do the right thing. It is essentially your north star.

Gentleness is translated as "usefulness." When we lose our gentleness, we become useless to God and others. Usefulness always precedes kindness. We are salt and light. If our salt gets contaminated, we venture off into the territory of good for nothingness.

Arguing, fussing, and fighting in a relationship is no good, especially if It is a fight to be correct. No one is 100% right all the time. No one, and I mean no one.

In every relationship, there will be disagreements. It's okay to disagree; just do not become disagreeable, so much so the folks across the street have to call the police! When this happens, it destroys your Christian witness.

Moreover, without kindness, we cannot go on to goodness. The Lord's interpretation of our usefulness and influence was dichotomized into his salt and light message.

As believers, we are called to be salt and light. Salt was precious during the ministry of Jesus. Roman soldiers were sometimes paid with salt. Salt tastes the same whether in Soweto, South Africa, London, England, or a country town in rural Alabama. Salt adds flavor to food. It makes it more palatable, and salt keeps the meat from spoiling. It has preservative properties.

When we are salty, it keeps us from being wishy-washy. If you are not salted, your spouse will think they are married to Jekyll and Hyde. Be a salty spouse and add some flavor and preservative to the relationship, guaranteeing it will last.

Salt sanitizes as well as preserves. Amazingly, salt is a poison made up of sodium and chloride. Now, if they are consumed separately, it could cause a fatality. However, we consume salt without thinking about its composition because God can take the poison out of it!

Furthermore, Jesus says we are light. Light travels at a speed of 186,000 miles per second. The master saw the light as an essential product in our lives. When salt manifests itself, it won't be very long before light will appear and dispel the darkness.

Matthew 5:13-16

[13] "You are the salt of the earth. But how can the salt be made salty again if it loses its saltiness? It is no longer good for anything except to be thrown out and trampled underfoot.

¹⁴ You are the light of the world. A town built on a hill cannot be hidden. ¹⁵ Neither do people light a lamp and put it under a bowl. Instead, they put it on its stand, and it gives light to everyone in the house. ¹⁶ Similarly, let your light shine before others so they may see your good deeds and glorify your Father in heaven."

6. Goodness needs no explanation. Being good and doing good is just good. It's just nice to be nice. Goodness is avoiding evil and always striving to do the right thing. Goodness allows you to overcome offenses. We should never be offended by the truth. In fact, we are made free by hearing the truth. In marriage, many things will be said intentionally and unintentionally that can cause friction and cause sparks to fly off the anvil of our mouths. Sometimes, hatred and even betrayal may raise its ugly head. However, goodness allows you to stop pointing fingers and look at yourself honestly. Am I the cause of this mess? Self-inventory is the best inventory.

Romans 12:10 "Be kindly affectioned one to another with brotherly love; in honor preferring one another;" King James Version (KJV).

I have seen couples get bent all out of shape when it appears one is moving up in status and starts making more money. The local paper may even print a news spread on them. Instead of celebrating upward mobility in oneness and solidarity, it becomes a battle for intimidation, which is silly and should not be. Husband and wife should celebrate each other's success. When one succeeds, you both succeed, amen!

Joshua 1:18 "This book of the law shall not depart out of thy mouth, but thou shalt meditate therein day and night, that thou mayest observe to do according to all that is written therein: for then thou shalt make thy way prosperous, and then thou shalt have good success."

Galatians 6:9-10 "Let us not become weary in **doing good** (*kalos*), for at the proper time we will reap a harvest if we do not give up."

7. Meekness This virtue gives no evidence of a self-inflated ego and shows humility at every opportunity. It's having a down-to-earth attitude without one's head in the clouds because of one's looks or achievements. Without God, we can do nothing. **(John 15:5)**

When people show meekness, they are usually low-key and work behind-the-scenes kind of person. They show humility, are never boastful, and have a teachable spirit. The worst student in the class is a know-it-all; "Tell em pastor" is their go-to statement. They always position themselves above or more advanced than the other students. I have taught classes where a know-it-all-all is in the class, and they talk all over themselves, and if left to run free, they will become a wreck on the road.

If you know everything there is to know about God and you are constantly interrupting bible class or a spiritual setting, you are a good candidate for heaven because that's where you belong. You know it all, and there is no room for growth. There I said It! Stop it; we all are on the potter's wheel, and there is room for improvement in our lives.

We will never know it all regardless of how long we have been in the kingdom. Even when we arrive in heaven, we will still be disciples learning more about the eternal truths of God and His Word!

Meekness manifests when a person does not take offense to the jabs. Sometimes, it may cause you to suffer an embarrassing moment. But even in the midst of that, as Rudyard Kipling so eloquently said, you can "walk with kings and not lose the common touch."

Matthew 11:29 "Take My yoke upon you and learn from Me, for I am gentle and lowly in heart, and you will find rest for your souls."

8. Faithfulness is having trust, confidence, steadfastness, and superb reliability. This fruit allows us to enjoy sweet fellowship with the Father. Faithfulness causes us to realize that all that we have belongs to God. Every couple must see that their material goods are not their own but God's blessings under our stewardship. When we are faithful, this opens many doors to more incredible blessings.

Faithfulness is being faithful to your vows before man, angels, and God. We generally see infidelity as running around on the husband or the wife. But it is running around on God!

Faithfulness further involves being faithful to our family, church, and service to the kingdom. Faithfulness is faith in our secular work and stewardship.

9. Self-control is the ability to control one's emotions, sexual desires, and will. It is the discipline of an athlete to run a race and stay the course.

Titus: 1:7-8 "Since an overseer manages God's household, he must be blameless—not overbearing, not quick-tempered, not given to drunkenness, not violent, not pursuing dishonest gain. Rather, he must be hospitable, loving what is good, self-controlled, upright, holy, and disciplined."

Temperance is the KJV rendered. The Greek word, according to the lexicon

Egkrateia (eng-krat-i-ah), which means "self-control" or "continence."

It is also derived from the Greek word *"Kratos."*

The fruit of the spirit is the ultimate characteristic that men and women should look for in a wholesome relationship. These qualities are Christ. They show the maturity of the individual to be Christlike and are visible and should manifest in every believer's life. They do not have to be taught to a person; they come naturally and automatically. When this happens, the marriage relationship will have its proper balance.

These qualities are a sign that the Holy Spirit is an active agent in your spouse's life.

There are four functions of self-control they are **mastery over idolatry, mastery over fornication,** and **mastery over tempting the Lord** and **complaining**. Israel was diseased with all four, and Samson had his challenges as well. Paul admonished us to be cured of them all.

See 1 Corinthians 10

First, God will have no other God before Him. We cannot serve the god of money, the god of political parties, the god of fame, and even the gods of our spouses, our children, as well as our possessions.

The golden calf must be destroyed. **(Exodus 32)**

Secondly, mastery over fornication should be pursued because we are called to live a holy and consecrated life. We have been bought with a price. **1 Corinthians 6:20** and **1 Corinthians 10:8.**

Thirdly, we must gain mastery over tempting the Lord or pushing God to act by putting ourselves in a compromising position. We must never seek to push God. God is not a God that can be pushed anyway. Judas tried to push Jesus; Judas thought if he could put Christ in the wrong position with the Romans, this would hasten the kingdom's coming. Boy, he sure did get it wrong. To escape embarrassment, he killed himself after his plan failed. You cannot push God to do anything.

God does not work by time; He works by eternity.

When a woman marries a man, she changes her name. This is a spiritual transfer. This act means that the woman has agreed to come under the care, custody, and control of the man, who is head of the union. The man's headship is Christ. The husband is the head of the wife, as Christ is the head of the Church.

Ephesians 5:23 "For the husband is the head of the wife, even as Christ is the head of the church: and he is the savior of the body."

If the husbands are not mindful of this robust duty of being a husband.

And the relationship with the wife is not Christlike and is abusive. God will not hear your cries, and your prayers will be hindered.

1Peter 3:1-7 "In the same way, you husbands must give honor to your wives. Treat your wife with understanding as you live together. She may be weaker than you are, but she is your equal partner in God's gift of new life. Treat her as you should so your prayers will not be hindered."

Fourth, self-control keeps you from being a chronic nagger, always complaining about everything and never coming to the point of satisfaction. In reality, this makes your spouse "perform" all the time. Marriage is not a talent show; it is a mutual life of love unconditionally, warts and all.

The children of Israel were long on complaining and short on appreciation. Whatever your mate does, always show some appreciation. It may not be what you expected, but act like you care and appreciate the effort. I used to buy my wife clothes, but it never met her expectations. So I just give her cash! That always wins the day.

Moses had a congregation that complained about everything. They wore him down so much that he blew his cool and missed the blessed trip of entering the promised land. Don't let complaining stop God's blessing on your home. You will miss out on a lot from God if you constantly complain.

A story is told concerning a lady who died and went to heaven. Upon her arrival, Peter flew her around on an angel's back. The ride was so smooth that she hardly knew she was moving; they came to a warehouse full of boxes. She spotted her name and asked Peter, "Why do those rows of boxes have my name on them?" Peter replied, "My child, I promise you don't want to know." She pressed him even further, so he finally said,

"Those boxes are the blessings God told the shipping department to cancel because you complained." Let us be grateful and watch God open the windows of heaven and send us unbelievable blessings.

1 Corinthians !0:9 "We must not put Christ[a] to the test, as some of them did and were destroyed by serpents, **10 nor grumble**, as some of them did and were destroyed by the Destroyer."

The fruit basket of the spirit in the home will cause the husband and wife to grow to maturity and be a blessing to one another. Take time to grow and develop into adulthood and the full stature of Jesus Christ. **(Ephesians 4:3)**

Chapter Eleven

Becoming A Five Star Spouse

In our contemporary society, markets and worldwide competition hold significant sway. Any item that has market value or is available for purchase undergoes evaluation by various agencies or regulatory entities.

Airlines are rated for quality of service, and Skytrax benchmarks them. Automobiles are tested for quality, reliability, customer feedback, and recalls, to mention a few by JD Power. Schools are rated based on student achievement, enrollment, retention, gainful employment, and teacher qualifications for accreditation purposes. Even the movie industry has its unique rating organization, the Motion Picture Industry of America, or MPAA. Appliances and power equipment, too, have rating bodies.

As a single person looking for a relationship, your desirability matters. Though it may sound vain, your "rating" impacts your chances of finding a partner. You become "off the market" when you get engaged or married. So don't brush off concerns about your appeal. Take steps to be the best version of yourself. Your relationship status can instantly change if you attract the right person.

You are marketing a product. It is the whole of you. The sale's success depends on what real estate agents call "staging." Houses are staged to look lived in and made to allow the shopper to see what the house looks like as a home with them in it. It's all about what they can imagine. Now, let that soak in for a minute.

When you go out to dinner, and the waiter brings your plate, everything looks so good and orderly. It only gets jumbled up after you start eating. The orderly arrangement is called "presentation." Similarly, you are on the market when you are single and searching. Your "staging" and "presentation" make all the difference. You are out to make yourself the "dish" to be desired. Your goal is to get ordered and jumbled up! Excuse my dining-out analogy; it's how the spirit reveals to me.

When you are on the market, it's how you dress, your style, intellect, haircut, hairdo, and your unique persona.

You must see where you stand if you will be the best you can be for your spouse. Good restaurants keep building clientele and keep them coming back for more. You must build momentum and keep your prospective spouse returning for more because they love what you do. That said, what's your score? How would you rate yourself? Analyze what you have to offer.

Hotels are classed from 1 to 5 stars. It is an international rating system that helps consumers determine the type of quality and amenities to expect with their stay. The higher the rating, the better the experience and the higher the cost of your stay. Personally, the highest-rated hotel I have ever stayed in was the Gaylord Resort in Nashville, Tennessee. It is a 4-star hotel. I was so overwhelmed by the scale and size of the property. It can be quite intimidating to navigate, especially if this is your first experience on the property. It is massive, boasting 3000 guest rooms and a water park inside. It is unreal. Restaurants are everywhere, with enough variety to satisfy any taste and budget.

Every spouse should want to put their shine on and be the best partner they can become. There are certain levels of excellence that we all should strive to meet. Let's explore the framework of the 1 to 5-star hotel rating system and see if we can look at what we do in our relationships. Let's see what it would take to upgrade and move up to being a 5-star spouse, which is the ultimate lap of love and luxury.

"The Manual" This online magazine helps us to understand the hotel rating systems better:

One star: They are budget facilities that are clean and secure. Guests can access fee-based services or facilities such as the Internet and pay on-demand movies in their rooms. Just somewhere to lay your head. It may be in an undesirable environment.

Two stars: Appeals to price-driven travelers, services and facilities are typically limited, there is little flash, no pool on the property, and Wi-Fi is usually free.

Three stars: A broad range of amenities and exceedingly above-average accommodation needs are available. Service and design are of good quality. A pool spa can be found and offer a hot breakfast; some may offer Happy Hour, and a fitness center is open during certain hours.

Four stars: Comes with a wide range of facilities, superior stylish design qualities, and excellent services. These hotels offer a deluxe guest experience—all the above plus more. The rooms are more extensive (square footage with nicer perks)—upscale bathroom fixtures and closet. Small appliances are the norm.

Five stars: Guests enjoy an extensive range of facilities and comprehensive services. The properties are well-designed and maintained.

Attention to detail: Luxury is visible across all areas of hotel operations, and service is obvious. Rooms fit the bill as expensive, sporting marble tops and floors in the bath area. Beds are uniquely made with freshly laundered bedsheets, and it has an inviting flare. In other words, they are upscale.

So, what does a **Star Ranked Spouse** look like? Let me make a disclaimer: This is my interpretation after years of observation as a pastor and is not based on empirical data. Here it goes ...

One-Star Spouse: You may ask what a 1-star spouse relationship looks like. A spouse does the bare minimum to keep from getting run off! They come home after work, put their clothes in the right place, and always do things cheaply. It's never anything beyond the basics to survive. There are no movies, shopping, or recreation; it's a burger, pizza, or dinner from the local Deli. Paying the bills and keeping the lights, water, gas, and cable on is the priority. Prefers to split rent or mortgage. Resting on the couch, and maybe a little romance on a Wednesday or a Friday, especially when they feel horny. It is doing just enough to keep from getting put out. The wardrobe may come from Walmart or Dirt Cheap. Drive basic transportation to get from point A to point B.

Attends church at least once a month, if at all. Preferably, on Sunday, their favorite choir sings. Groceries are inventoried at a minimum, lunch meat to make sandwiches, and enough meat and potatoes for a complete meal once a week. Beer or ClubTail Margaretta on weekends if desired. Preowned cars for husband and wife to drive. The wife does her hair and may cut the husband's as well. Not much cooking goes on in the house, especially on weekends.

Two Star Spouses: You must have a big screen TV, put clothes up. They do a little more than the bare minimum to stay in the house. They will help in cleaning up. They come home from work, and they get off work after an hour or so. They will set up a budget, be willing to go out occasionally, dress on average, wear a fragrance, have minimum shopping, and maybe a gym membership. Eat out at least once a month. The wife does her hair; the husband visits the barber weekly. A wife is usually the one who attends children's extracurricular activities.

They share the cost of utilities, like electricity, gas, and water, as well as cable and housing expenses. They seldom go to church. Shows affection verbally and touch teasing. A refrigerator is average stocked. They hang out with friends on weekends. Little sex and romance only agreed upon days.

Alcohol use is above average. The cars people drive are often new. Typically, the man of the house takes care of the yard work.

Three Star Spouse: They have multiple entertainment systems in the home. Netflix is a must. They put clothes up and fold them sometimes. They will do above average to stay in the house, do yard work, follow a budget, come home immediately after work, wear fragrance, walk for exercise, attend church regularly, and may hold a leadership position in the church. They are also romantic and playful. Friends visit the house occasionally. They plan short trips for the family and are a good communicator. The wife does her hair but attends hair salons for special occasions. The husband visits the barbershop every other week. Sex is spontaneous and may happen without planning or notice.

They own better-than-average cars for both spouses to use. A few high-end vehicles are parked in the garage. He buys her some fine jewelry to wear. They might also have a pet, like a dog or a cat.

Four Star Spouses: This couple enjoys a luxurious lifestyle, complete with a home theater and designer fashion. While the husband isn't typically romantic, he does make spontaneous romantic gestures and usually initiates them. He also handles household chores like washing dishes and folding laundry but leaves financial management entirely to his wife. They are active church members and may even hold significant leadership roles there. The husband often gives his wife and kids money for shopping. Family vacations are a regular event for them. They drive high-end cars like Lexus and Mercedes and live in above-average homes. The wife frequents the salon but might do her own touch-ups, while the husband gets a haircut every week or two. Their intimate moments are usually well-planned, often after dinner or a night out.

Home-cooked meals are done primarily by the wife. Either the wife or children wash dishes.

They may own a business or are partner in one. The home will likely have a part-time maid or housekeeper and a paid lawn service. Homes will likely have custom cabinets and expensive appliances. Pets are the norm. A dog, cat, or bird may be on the property to entertain the children.

Five Star Spouse: The family enjoys a home movie theater and owns luxury wardrobe items, including Christian Louboutin shoes for both men and women. They employ a part-time housekeeper and have an accountant for tax matters. The wife manages the daily finances. Their family name holds significant social prestige. The couple brings in a six-figure income, and the wife either doesn't work or runs her own business. Regular family vacations are a staple; while the wife's shopping is modest, it's consistent. They are active churchgoers and hold leadership roles. They attend professional sports events at least annually and might even have season tickets. The wife frequents the hair and nail salon as she pleases, while the husband gets a weekly haircut and wears the latest high-end cologne. Custom dress shirts with cufflinks and their name embroidered are standard attire.

Sex and romance are usually initiated by the wife by the way she dresses. Husband likes to golf and keeps up with the latest sports; he may coach a little league team or be a sponsor. Family vacations and getaways are an annual event. The husband gives the wife a shopping allowance at her discretion.

The wife or husband cooks exotic meals that sometimes are showstoppers, and the dishwasher handles the dishes.

Their home is located in a posh neighborhood, and it is one of a kind. The house will likely have high-end appliances and customized cabinets. Even their vehicles are expensive. Professional lawn service is utilized. Pets are the norm on the property.

So, you are wondering what you can do to up your game. There are so many things to consider in establishing a home. Is there something that flies under the radar that seems to be insignificant? The answer is yes. Briefly, let me suggest two things: colors and music. You heard me right; they are colors and music.

As you start your married life together, think about a consistent color theme for your home. Your home is your sanctuary, and the colors influence your behavior in ways that will greatly surprise you. As a sociology major, I am just fascinated with what influences society and trends.

The U.S. Justice Department conducted a study in 1992 on how colors affect inmates' behavior. I know you are not an inmate, but the Justice Department found that red causes a rise in heart rate, breathing, and other nervous system functions more than green or blue. Orange and yellow had a more calming, warm effect. Green makes time appear to be condensed and shorter. Decorate your sanctuary to create the atmosphere you desire. That said, colors and your positive issues of outcome also matter. Take it for what it's worth.

Lastly, music is another thing to consider if you want to improve your game and the atmosphere as a spouse. If you shop in various stores, you will notice that the music is classic, soft, and sophisticated in high-end fashion stores. On the other hand, when you enter a teenyboppers store, the music is loud and thumping. Different music appeals to the age and sets the tone or atmosphere that affects sales.

Your home should reflect your style in music and color. These small things can impact your road to becoming a 5-star spouse!

Chapter Twelve

He That Findeth a Wife

Nine Biblical Keys to Discovery: The Isaac Model

In Proverbs 18:22, the Bible says, "Whoso findeth a wife findeth a good thing, and obtaineth favor of the Lord."

There are **(9) keys or steps** to finding a wife or the ideal mate according to the biblical model found in **Genesis 24**. Let us look at the story that leads to successful search and find. As we glide through each step, you should see the difference between Eleazar's and Samson's choices. Notice the glaring differences throughout the 9-step process. Samson's choices led to disaster, and Eleazar's choices led to success. This is how you can get right what you keep getting wrong while you are single and searching.

Now, Isaac is a beautiful love story that is positive in all aspects. It is a romance that is real and unfolds like a fairytale. Ultimately, a beautiful woman becomes Cinderella because she fits perfectly in Eleazar's mission and the answer to his prayer.

Each key found in the search for a bride for Isaac builds on the other.

Historically, Isaac is the son of Promise and the eligible bachelor in question. Abram is the first patriarch mentioned in scripture from the Ur of the Chaldees. In time, he marries his half-sister Sari, who is barren. God promised Abram he would be a Father of many nations and extended his name to Abraham. Nevertheless, it appears time is running out in his old age because he and his wife are still childless. So, he decides to have a son with his wife's handmade Hagar. Ishmael is born not the son of Promise but rather the son of the flesh.

Nevertheless, about 13 years later, his wife had a son—Isaac. As the redemptive drama unfolds, Abraham sees the sun setting in his life. But before he dies, he wants to find a bride for his son Isaac. Therefore, he sends a servant to Mesopotamia, to Nahor. While not named, the servant is most likely Eleazar. Eleazar is sent to Abraham's relatives' hometown to find a bride. The servant does what he was commissioned to do, nothing more and nothing less. But how would he accomplish this? Let's examine God's blueprint that led Abraham's servant to success.

Eleazar is a type of Holy Spirit, and the bride-to-be is Rebekah, a kind of Church; Isaac is a type of Jesus Christ, and Abraham, of course, is a type of God the Father.

Before we walk through the keys, consider the journey, the jewel, and the joy.

The Journey- Finding a wife is described as a journey, a pursuit, or a search. She must be discovered, which suggests it is a challenging task. Just as a good man is hard to find, so is a good woman.

Notice that the word findeth is repeated twice, and the word obtaineth is recorded only once. You should strive twice as hard to find a mate and hold on to her. When the Lord, by his providence, places the love of your life in your hands, you will indeed hold on to her. Furthermore, "findeth" suggests brisk and continuous pursuit until she is found. If you at first do not succeed, try again.

The Jewel- When a wife is found, she is precious like a jewel. Like a precious jewel that is unearthed, she is at last found. She shines like a gemstone suspended in the prongs of eternity. The rays of her love will shine forever.

The Joy- When a wife is found, it produces God's favor and joy, especially in the heart of the one who is searching and the heart of the one who is found in that search.

It is a sign that God has endorsed the union and showered his blessing upon it. Although unseen, God attends every wedding he approves, and His hand of blessings places his stamp of approval.

Consider the keys:

Genesis 24 Key #1 The Prohibition: The servant is not to take a wife from the Canaanites but only from Abraham's own compatriots and family. In one's search, one should set boundaries on what one will and will not accept. What market will you seek a mate? Church venue, school, workplace, and other social events. Where will you not be looking for a mate? Strip Club? Bars? Street corners? Church? Does nationality matter? Does religious preference matter? What are the prohibitions? Establish a fence, and search should only be within the parameters of the fence. In everyone's journey, there's always that "Wet Paint: Do Not Touch" sign. It's like life's way of saying, "Nice try, but hands off!"

Many people are recreational smokers today. With the acceptance of marijuana, will you accept a mate who abuses drugs? What about the work schedule? Do you want a mate who is at home when you are off work? Many prohibitions must be considered before there is a deep dive.

On the contrary, Samson broke all the prohibitions related to family norms. The most alarming was his Nazarite vows. These vows were the staples that would have held his life and his anointing together.

Key #2 v 4 verse The Father Chooses. If we truly believe in the sovereignty of God, we will have faith to believe that God has our lifelong wife or husband already marked out for us. Since God made us, he knows our innermost thoughts and can place in our path the most compatible person who will complement us, and we can complement them. We have strengths and weaknesses, credits and liabilities, and God's choice can turn our liabilities into excelling assets.

I believe God has that special someone already for you. If marriage is your dream, God has a unique way of causing time, providence, and destiny to meet at the right time. God is sovereign, and he is in control. Let God work things out on your behalf.

Psalm 85:10-13 "Steadfast love and faithfulness meet; righteousness and peace kiss each other. Faithfulness springs from the ground and righteousness looks down from the sky. Yes, the Lord will give what is good, and our land will yield its increase. Righteousness will go before him and make his footsteps a way."

Key #3 The Portfolio The servant takes ten of his master's camels. This was only a preview of what his master owned. Abraham was rich. Isaac was the son of a rich man who stood to inherit all that his father owned. I don't know any girl looking for a broke man to marry! All that the servant had was in his stewardship. What do you have in your portfolio that will become building blocks for a strong marriage? Is it a promising career, good looks, Christian character, religious upbringing, a good education, real estate, money, a sold-out life for God, or goals? What do you bring to the table? What does your portfolio look like?

I suggest that if you do not have any money or many assets but you have a dream and goals, that is more than enough to go places in life. My wife married me not because of what I had but because of what I had the potential to become. My parents left me with real estate holdings. She never found out about it until later in our relationship. I wanted to ensure our love was not because of what I had but because she felt we could accomplish great things with the Lord's guidance and blessings.

Key #4 Prayer v 12-13 The servant prayed that God would grant him success in his undertaking and that the prospective bride would be revealed. Prayer moves the hand of God in our lives. When we ask God to enter our situation, he performs the miraculous. In the field of algebra, there are variables in the equation. If you happen to change the variables, you change the outcome. Likewise, you will always have a positive effect whenever you include Jesus in the equation of life.

Matthew 6:33: "But seek ye first the kingdom of God, and His righteousness, and all these things shall be added unto you."

When we pray, we should pray that God's will be done in our lives. Kindergarten teachers have difficulty training a child to stay within the lines. They struggle because of their poor motor skills or not fully developed. It's hard to stay within the lines of a horse in a coloring book. The crayon sometimes does not seem to cooperate.

We begin with the end in our mind. Always be mindful to stay within the lines of God's perfect will; if we do, we will have the desires of our hearts. Eleazar knew how to ask God for what he wanted because he began with the end in mind.

Ask, seek, and knock, and it will be opened unto you. **Matthew 7:7-8**

Pray about everything. Celebrate God's goodness and always seek wisdom from God. Wisdom is a skill. The fear of God is the beginning of wisdom. Wisdom is personified in scripture as a woman who stands in the streets and points the way. There are so many directions we can choose. Only the Lord knows the most productive paths and the most productive people that will make a difference in our lives. The right one is only a prayer away.

The Chinese bamboo tree is a fantastic plant in botany. The first couple of years you water and fertilize it, nothing happens regarding its growth. However, something incredible happens in the fifth year; each week, it grows higher, and in 5 more weeks, it shoots up to 90 feet tall! Real love takes time; it will appear and extend beyond imagination over time.

Key #5 v14-17 Providence: Providence comes from the word that means to see before in advance. "Pro" means before, in the Greek "evidence" is where we get the word video. God knows all things because of his foreknowledge and the servant asks for God's Choice to manifest by doing specific things as a sign for him. God's providence brings people and events together. The Wise men in the Birth of Jesus narrative all had the same dream not to return to Herod but to go home another way. That is indeed providence. God saw in advance that Herod had evil intentions.

Samson's life seldom reflected God's guidance; he always concocted his plans, which inevitably hit a dead end.

The coyote in the cartoon the "Road Runner," always comes up with some contraption to attempt to outsmart the Road Runner, but he gets outfoxed every time. It's best to let God run our lives and order our steps. After all, he made us and knows all about us. **(Psalm 37:33)**

In addition, the life of Joseph is an excellent example of providence. He was sold into slavery by his jealous brothers over a beautiful coat of many colors. That coat today would look like the jackets Michael Jackson wore. It was a sequin garment, or jewel-like in appearance, that glittered with the sun's rays. Joseph ended up in Potiphar's house and became chief steward over all his master had. Handsome and lied to by his master's wife, he was thrown in jail. Eventually, his ability to interpret dreams brought him before the Pharaoh's throne. He became vice-president of Egypt, riding second in the King's motorcade. It was designed to preserve his people from the famine in the land and assure that the seed of Abraham, Jesus Christ, would come. It is called providence. What God has to do to get you and that significant other to the same spot is providence.

Providence is a word that means "to see before" or "to see in advance." God sees our past, present, and future all at the same time. If we allow the Spirit of God to lead us, we cannot and will not go wrong.

Key #6 v16-20 Productivity/Work Ethic: Rebekah is the girl of Promise. A beautiful virgin girl shows up. She shows hospitality, kindness, productivity, and servanthood by giving him something to drink and going the extra mile; she waters all ten camels! She is not lazy but industrious, and it shows love in the most profound sense.

Work builds character. Rebekah showed that she was a woman of Industry, and her home would be a place of love, beauty, and productivity when one's ingenuity, innovation, and imagination come together. A life of courtship is a bouquet of creativity that changes the atmosphere of any dull place.

God told Adam and Eve to be fruitful and multiply. God expects humanity to be productive, and where there is hate, leave love, and where there is nothing, be sure that something worthwhile is left behind. Like Rebekah, go the extra mile. Be more, do more.

Key #7 v 21-27 Reflection/Discernment: The servant surveyed all that had taken place and evaluated all that his physical and spiritual senses could pick up until he was convinced that God had given him the success he desired. Marriage is an essential thing and must be seen through the lenses of the physical and the spiritual. The servant got his confirmation. Samson never stopped to reflect on his actions, and as a result, he never considered changing his ways.

Key #8 28-51, 60 Parental/Family Blessing: Rebekah was so excited because she discovered the purpose of the servant's journey to her house. After her family was filled in on the details, they agreed. Couples that do not receive the blessings of their family are in for a rocky ride. Marriage brings families together, and if one side of the family despises the other, it will be hell to pay as you struggle to live together. Samson never received those blessings from his family; they just went along to get along. Sad, but so true.

Prince Harry and Meghan Markle have had a rocky relationship with the Royals since their wedding plans were announced. The gossip tabloids have all reported a rift between the Queen and Harry's family. Try to get into a harmonious relationship with the families involved. This will make for a smooth blending or an unhappy ending. Marriage in the East is considered not a joining of a couple but rather the joining of a family and community.

God wants to bless us beyond our wildest dreams. Man plans his way, but God directs his steps. We never know how God is going to bless us. His ways are unlimited and come in all directions and various forms.

I remember planning an anniversary trip for me and my wife to Memphis for a weekend at the Peabody. It would be capped off with barbeque at the *Rendezvous,* and carriage rides around downtown Memphis. I booked a room on the VIP floor, hoping to see famous ball players of the Grizzlies or even some movie stars in town for a getaway. But things went wrong after we arrived.

We checked in and went to my room, but the room was occupied! I was so outdone and disappointed. I told the *maître d,* and she asked what the occasion was. I said our wedding anniversary. She said, "Oh, my goodness. We have messed up." So, she stepped away, gave me a complimentary bottle of wine, and sent for the manager. He comes and apologizes and gives me another key for accommodations on another floor, not the VIP floor. I object, but the manager says I think you will like it, and if you don't, let me know, and I will fix it.

So here we go on the elevator, down to another floor to another room. Walking the long hall, we eventually arrive at a room with a gold embossed plaque that says, "W.C. Handy Suite." We enter, and wow, it's a whole house with a kitchen, a dining room, a hallway, an office, a living room, a large bedroom, and a jacuzzi. They messed it up so God could bless me! God wants the best for us; if we let God do it, it will always be well done. God blessed a village girl named Rebekah. This probably was not what she signed up for, and it looks like a blind date mess, but in the end, it's a great blessing.

KEY #9 Genesis 24:50-58 The Engagement/Faith: Bethuel saw that the Lord was in the plan and received the dowry. Rebekah received her gifts. The deal was sealed, and it was now time to go and meet her groom, Issac. Rebekah was asked, **"Will you go with this man?"** Rebekah said, **"I will go!"** Rebekah was willing to make this her choice; she was ready to change her surroundings to a new land, and she was willing to commit to a man she had never seen. This beautifully captures our embrace of Jesus. The Holy Spirit gives the whole world an invitation to follow him. Will you go with this man? Will you leave your waterpots of the old life, and after you meet him will you tell others about the joy and the happiness you have found **(John 4:27-30)**

Let's face it: Rebekah had absolutely no idea what she was getting herself into. It was a faith walk. I guess you say, what experience do you have in all this? My wife and I have been married for 35 years, and I am still trying to figure out what I have gotten myself into. It's a faith walk. I still can't figure out why she is still around, and I don't think I have improved. God's grace is the only explanation I can come up with.

Meanwhile, Rebekah goes with the servant to meet a man who was most likely described to her. It was all an exercise in faith. Marriage and proper courtship is a faith walk. "For we walk by faith and not by sight." (2 Cor 5:7). How does the story end? Genesis 24 says that they hurried to meet when they saw each other. In Gen. 24:67, the Bible says he took her to be his wife, and he loved her. Faith believes even when we don't see it. This is a beautiful picture of the church's marriage to Christ. We know we will see him and be with him even though we have not seen it yet, but we wait eagerly to finally meet the one who loved us and died for us.

Samson and his Women, as recorded in the book of Judges (Chapters 13-16), is a must-read for every single individual searching for their spouse. It challenges our morals, standards, and the opinions of others and causes us to evaluate what matters to God and not our selfish, sensual-driven inclinations.

Now, regardless if you are a Christian, a non-Christian, an atheist, or an agnostic. We all want to get it right. If you are going to get married and live with someone until death, do your part; it would serve you well to be with someone who will complement and enhance your very existence.

Samson was a ladies' man right off the cover of GQ Magazine. He loved to live his life outside the margins. If we could say anything tremendous and glorious about Sunny Boy, it would be that he was consistent. Consistent in doing everything imaginable contrary to the Covenant of God and the Nation of Israel. Samson was consistent. He did the same thing in choosing girlfriends from the enemy camp. He expected a different result by doing the same thing repeatedly. It was insanity.

The jury is still out over finding lasting relationships through social media and various online dating platforms. God's design is simple. Interpersonal relationships are the mothership to a genuine love without the drama. A simple date or a night out in the town will allow any couple to gather sufficient information to determine if further investment in time, touch, and treasury will be beneficial and lead to marriage.

Moreover, this writer intended to leave you with a GPS leading out of the maze of Samson's senseless adventures. The Story of Isaac gives us a beautiful Mosaic as a picture of Christ and the enormous effort He displayed to show us his love. I pray that you find His Love sufficient and His Godly and timely principles of love that will lead to a satisfying and productive lifelong relationship.

If you are into getting scientific data to understand yourself in your single and searching journey, may I suggest the Myers-Briggs Test that allows you to explore four key areas: how you use and direct your energy, how you process information, how you come to conclusions and lastly how you approach the outside world.

Another instrument of note is Truity. It is kind of a companion to Myers-Briggs and boasts of telling you who you really are. This personality test gives you some idea of your ideal dream partner. Try it and see if you like what you find out. Enjoy and trust God, and have fun on your journey!

Chapter Thirteen

To Be or Not to Be

Well, you have seen most of the pitfalls of Samson and his women and the secrets to successful marriage life and relationship. It is up to you to determine whether you want to get married. Always know who you are getting married to; that decision should always be about love. It should not be because you got pregnant, your spouse had a financial windfall, you wanted to leave your parent's house, or your fiancé promised a big, fine, cozy home. It must always happen because you are in love. There is a Tyler Perry's play adapted to TV starring Janet Jackson in "**Why Did I Get Married**." If you are unfamiliar with this flick, I strongly recommend it as your personal consultant and counselor. Many objective life truths are played out on the big screen.

Four couples that have been best friends since college decided to retreat in the mountains; it's a kind of spur-of-the-moment thing with very little organization. Their relationships have all been dysfunctional, and they get to re-assess "Why they decided to get married" and come to startling conclusions.

There is no need to find yourself in a situation where you are trying to determine what the HE Double Hockey Stick (**Hell**) happened, and you jump your tail off into the skillet.

To be or not to be is the question asked in Hamlet, Act 3, by Prince Hamlet, where he contemplates death and suicide as he surveys the unfairness of life. You must decide if you want to be married or not. That is the question. It would help if you considered your age. Have you reached the point in your life where you are mature enough and ready to take on the responsibility of marriage? Are you too young, or are you too old? What considerations are necessary to assess the amount of change and compromise you might need to make the marriage become a success? What habits have you picked up that could hinder your marriage success? Do you still love to party and hang out with your friends? Do you spend and waste too much money? Are you guilty of having a harem of significant others in your imagination that you refuse to let go of, and if you get married, it could lead to a barrage of Infidelity?

Let me list a few things you should consider checking off your list. Remember that marriage is not a sprint. It is a long-distance run. Are you ready for a long-term commitment? When you say I do, it comes with tremendous considerations. Suppose you have been single for an extended period. You must be willing to give up some degree of freedom to do, come and go as you please. Marriage is a partnership, and it is not always a balanced transaction. Some schedules must be considered. Who will do the chores around the house? What will be your role? Who will pay the bills and keep up with the accounting aspect of the finances? What religion will you adhere to? Do you want children? What type of education do you prefer for them, public or private? Will you keep a gun in the home for protection? What kind of training will be required to discharge it if it becomes necessary safely?

Moreover, what are the necessary transitions you are willing to make to get married? Does your mate have children that will be brought into the marriage, and if so, how will they be blended into a new family structure? Questions run the gamut when it comes to having a successful marriage.

Data in the United States reveals that the average age for marriage is 29 for men and 27 for women. Another factor determining where it is "to be or not to be" is your attitude about marriage. When a man or a woman views marriage as bondage, and it offers no proper space for happiness and adventure, it is doomed from the start. At least from the beginning, the bride and the groom should have a favorable view of marriage if it is to have any chance of success.

The family background of your parents' marriage is also critical in how much baggage you unpack at the front door before putting all its contents inside. We model what we see, hear, and feel; if our parents' marriage ended in divorce, there is an even higher likelihood that yours will not fare so well. Now, do not be fearful if that is your family history. You want to drag in the best you saw in your parents' relationship and minimize the worst. You are building your own little kingdom, and you and your partner are the King and Queen of the castle. Leave as many biting alligators outside in the moat as you possibly can.

The biggest fight that couples have is over finance. Be sure you are ready to commit on an excellent financial footing. You will have peaceful, restful nights when your finances are in order.

I teach that all old bedroom furniture should be donated to someone else and never start a marriage with old beds from your wife's or husband's old life. This is a brand new life and brand-new living. You don't want memories of what used to be, but all about building on a good foundation. I will never forget my banker in Indianola, who long discussed this with me. I took it to heart because it was outside the purview of banking. He took a genuine interest in me and wanted me to have a great future. I include this in my pre-marriage counseling sessions. No couple should consummate a marriage without having their pastor, Rabbi, or a strong religious leader give them some biblical training on the fundamentals and expectations of marriage. It is invaluable.

In my earlier years of pastoring, I would marry a couple without counseling.

I do not perform weddings without the counseling part. If they don't have time for my counseling, I don't have time to complete the marriage. It may sound dogmatic, but I have the numbers to back it up.

Every couple that did not go through the counseling did not last. The couples that went through the counseling sessions stayed together!

My wife took a marriage class at our convention and could not wait to tell me the six purposes of marriage according to scripture. They are:

1. Companionship (Genesis 2:18, Genesis 2:24

2. Enjoyment (Hebrews 13:4)

3. Completeness (Genesis 2:23)

4. Fruitfulness (Genesis 1:28)

5. Protection (Ephesians (5:25, Titus 2:4-5)

6. Typify Christ and His Church (Ephesians 5:21-33)

When we understand the "why" or the purpose of marriage, we can quickly move toward the "how" of marriage. Satan's first step was to create distrust before the first couple could develop and understand God's purpose for them on the earth as an example to the world.

Trust is what destroyed Adam and Eve's relationship. They began to blame each other when they followed the serpent's direction. If a relationship has no trust in one area, there will be no trust in all areas.

Communication is another factor in how well you and your partner will succeed. Communication is the product of trust. Do you talk it out with reason? The Bible says we are to come together and reason together **(Isaiah1:18)**

Communication falls into (5) components that can be measured from ankle-deep to waist-deep. They are what I call:

A. Table Talk: What are we eating tonight, or where's the bread? Did you take the puppy out today? You say something only if you have to. It's small talk.

B. Street Level Talk: is what's the latest talk, gossip, from the street committee and upcoming events, and a plethora of casual chitchat.

C. The View from My Window: is a highly opinionated conversation. It could cover one's politics, the latest news, the Supreme Court's rulings, the legalization of weed, whether your daughter can go to the prom with her favorite guy, or wear that tight dress she ordered online.

D. Heart Talk: This talk is emotional and expresses our fears of acceptance and rejection. "Yesterday you hurt me when you said …," or "I want to know, do you really love me, or are you just playing around?" "Why won't you trust me with your bank PIN?" These are deeper conversations than the others because they can lead to heated confrontations.

E. Real Husband and Wife Talk: This type of talk is where you let your hair down, not dressing up the words; you just let it rip. It is an unconditional conversation where you and your spouse are transparent—just downright the naked truth. There are no reservations, and on this level, the bonds of matrimony grow physically, spiritually, and emotionally.

Finally, if you have prayed and asked for God's blessing and found Mr. or Ms. Right, and you have gotten the family blessing as seen in the Isaac model, you are good to go.

The Bible says, "Marriage is honorable in all, and the bed undefiled: but whoremongers and adulterers God will judge.

[5] Let your conversation be without covetousness, and be content with such things as ye have: for he hath said, I will never leave thee, nor forsake thee.

[6] So that we may boldly say, The Lord is my helper, and I will not fear what man shall do unto me." **Hebrews 13:4-6**

I pray that you have found the necessary tools and thought processing to assist you in your quest for a lifelong journey of a Spiritual relationship for a lifetime.

Chapter Fourteen

There Is a Silver Lining

It is very depressing when you find it hard to find anything positive in your life, and everything is running backwards. Samson proved that you could start good and end up wrong. All the women he encountered were not close to desirable. However, in the Bible, all women were not out to get you. All the women in Samson's life were indeed terrible loyalists. But there is a silver lining. Look at David. He also had some encounters with the Philistines but never was inclined to engage in romance. I want you to see how a Jewish girl treats her man. You can find someone who cares about you and will go the extra mile to love and protect you.

There is David and Michal. Now, David is no saint either. In time, he will have multiple wives at the same time. We find a ray of hope, as he is famous for defeating the giant Goliath. This is where David's troubles begin. David was King Saul's personal musician and armor bearer, and after he killed Goliath, his fame spread, and he had a number-one song on the billboard charts; the women sang, "Saul has killed his thousand and David his ten thousand." This made Saul so angry that he felt David was becoming a threat to his Kingship. Saul plans to marry David off to his daughter Michal, who openly admits she dearly loves David. This makes all the difference in the world.

In 1 Samuel 18: 20-21, Michal is Saul's youngest daughter, and David is Jessie's baby boy. Saul's daughter is more loyal to David than her father, Saul, who she knows is jealous, ruthless, and evil.

So, David, when presented with the idea of marriage, feels unworthy, as many men do when they compare their backgrounds with their girlfriends, which you should never do. David is surprised by Saul's proposal and states he is so poor that he cannot satisfy the price of claiming a bride with the desired dowry. Saul tells him to go and bring back 100 foreskins of the Philistines and bring them back to him. This would be the payment for his daughter. Nevertheless, Saul is really up to hoping David will get killed and at last he will be rid of him, and Saul's Kingship will be secure, so he thinks.

David more than meets the conditions and presents 200 foreskins, but the plan backfires on Saul. David called his bluff. Okay, here comes wicked plan number two. Saul sends men to David's house to kill David, but Michal, David's wife, finds out about it in advance, and David escapes due to her placing a decoy in the bed with goat's hair that looks like a body. The soldiers find out and are deceived. Saul is angry and gives Michal to another man! Sound familiar? It happened to Samson's girlfriend, number #1. She is given to Palti, son of Laish. David must have loved Michal because when he ascended to the throne of Judah, he took Michal back as his wife after all the necessary protocols were in place. **2 Sam 3: 13-15** says, "*And David* said, Good, I will make a covenant with you. But one thing I require of you: you shall not see my face unless you first bring Michal, Saul's daughter, when you come to see my face." [14] David sent messengers to Ishbosheth, Saul's son, saying, "Give *me* my wife Michal, whom I betrothed to myself for a hundred foreskins of the Philistines." [15] And Ishbosheth sent and took her from *her* husband, from [a]Palti, the son of Laish.

There is a silver lining behind every dark cloud in the quest for love; if we genuinely ask, seek, and knock, it shall be opened unto us. **(Matthew 7:7)**

In 1634, it was said that John Milton penned Every Cloud Has a Silver Lining in his poem **Comus: A Mask Presented at Ludlow Castle**, 1634:

I see ye visibly, and now believe.

That he, the Supreme Good, to whom all things ill

Are but as slavish officers of vengeance,

Would send a glistering guardian, if need were

To keep my life and honour unassailed.

Was I deceived, or did a sable cloud

Turn forth her **silver lining** on the night?

Suppose I could classify David's marriage to Saul's daughter. It would be like a Megan and Harry moment or a Michael Jackson and Lisa Marie Presley. It was a celebrity marriage on the front page of Judah's Magazine.

Many years ago, my church was looking for a piano. The church musician, Mr. Howell, and I went to a large music store to purchase a baby grand piano. Since I could play, I decided to test some models and hear how they sound. Amazingly, I played two pianos, which were side by side. One was sad, and the other was lively and bright. I was so surprised by the difference that I asked the salesman why there was such a sharp contrast. He stated that the pianos were hand-built. The sad-sounding piano was built by an engineer going through something traumatic. Whatever mood or state of mind an engineer is in transfers into the instrument. The salesman said, "There is no way to get that sadness or deadness out; it is built into the piano. The sadness in him can never be gotten out of the piano."

Whatever is in us affects everything we touch. We are to fill our lives with joy and happiness so that it permeates our homes and the people we love.

Regardless of how bad a relationship may look, some good can become of it. If God steps in, he can turn a mess into a miracle. If you have ever seen a boxing fight, if it appears that one of the boxers runs the risk of being severely hurt and is bloody and swollen, heading for a fatal blow. Knowing the fight should not proceed, the trainer throws a towel in the ring. This means stop the fight. Don't throw in the towel. Keep the faith.

I must admit that sometimes, couples want to throw in the towel in relationships. Always remember that when genuine love is present in a relationship, nothing can extinguish its flames. It may not always go as planned; you may be down but not out at some point. Behind every dark cloud, there is a silver lining. **(2 Cor 4:9)**

ENDNOTES

Chapter 1

1 Jessie Greenspan, "8 Things You may Not know about Superman." – February 6, 2023

2 Mahalia Jackson, "Without God I Could Do Nothing" written by B. Brown, PRU MUSIC PUBLISHING

3 Bride, Online Magazine "Hopeless Romantic"

November 16, 2022

4 Shlomo Chaim Kesselman, Chabad.Org,

"The Story of Samson and Delilah in the Bible"

Chapter 2

1 Tamar Kadari, "Jewish Woman Archives Women in Samson's Life": Midrash and Aggadah December 31, 1999

2 The Works of Flavius Josephus,Chapter "Concerning the Fortitude of Samson and What Mischief He Brough upon the Philistines".

Chapter 3

1 Spectrum Family Law, Money: "Financial Reasons Couples Get a Divorce" March – 15, 2023

2 Harry Reid, Las Vegas Sun: "The Time Has Come for Us to Outlaw Prostitution" – February 22, 2011

Chapter 5

1 Dominique Peruzzi, Statista: Cosmetics Sales Statistics - January 26, 2023

2 Paul Jackson, "Unmasking the Jezebel Spirit" Streams Publications - 2002

Chapter 6

1 Michael P. Green, *Illustrations* for Biblical Preaching

Grand Rapids, Mich, Baker Book House, 1990

2 Rick Warren, "4 Ways Envy Damages Your Life" Crosswalk. com - September 23, 2016

3 Illustration; "Tear Drops", About Bible.Org

Chapter 7

1 Mazeoflove.com, Online Dating Penetration Revenue in 2022 (829 million) in the United States

2 Dionysia Lemonak, "A Brief History of the Internet Who Invented It, How it Works and How it Became the Web We Use Today" - November 17, 2020

3 Pew Research Center, "The Virtues and Downsides of Online Dating" - October 16-28-2019

Chapter 8

Statista.com, "Advertising spent in the U.S." (Statistics & Facts)

Chapter 9

Michael K. Lake, Biblical Life College & Seminary, Master of Divinity Program Vol1, Lesson #4 "Fruit of the Spirit" - 1997

Chapter 11

1 Hotel Rating Systems, Hospitality.Com

Mike Richard, The Manuel: Online Publication, "How Do Hotel Star Rating Actually Work" January 26, 2021

2 U.S. Dept of Justice, Office of Justice Program

"Color and Its Effect on Inmate Behavior" -1992

3 Warner Brothers (Looney Tunes), Wile E. Coyote & The Road Runner

Chapter 13

1 Tyler Perry, "Why Did I get Married" (Comedy-Drama) 2007

2 Reverend Lovely and Nora Callaway "Ministering to Couples in the Local Church" Course#272 National Baptist Congress of Christian Education - June 19-23, 2000

All Scriptures are from The Holy Bible and are from various versions such as KJV, NKJ, NIV and NLT (www.BibleGateway.com)

Made in the USA
Monee, IL
12 March 2024

54892257R00075